Praise for *The New Parish*

"Something's up in neighborhoods right across this country. Kids raised in the generica of American suburbs are becoming adults who yearn deeply for a sense of place, for belonging, for community. *The New Parish* is a passionate call for churches to join in the beautiful work of placemaking, not only as a response to this yearning but as a core expression of the mission of God in our world." **Michael Frost**, author, *Incarnate*

"*The New Parish* offers us the needed framework to multiply and catalyze a movement that takes seriously the call of the community of God to our neighborhoods, cities and world." **Jon Huckins**, cofounder, The Global Immersion Project

"Strong communities, strongly rooted in place, are the future: for food, for energy, but also for our spiritual life. This is a powerful account of a necessary future." **Bill McKibben**, author, *Wandering Home*

"The idea and reality of a parish used to be geographical. Those called to lead . . . thanked God for the people in their neighborhood, put down roots, built relationships and incarnated the body of Christ. This book is an attempt to reclaim that traditional understanding in a new day for a new generation. It is much needed, and I am so thankful for it." The Rt. Rev. **Gregory H. Rickel**, VIII Bishop of Olympia

"If you cut Paul, Tim and Dwight, they bleed parish. The hope and integrity of the twenty-first-century Christian church may require that the rest of us learn to do the same." **Tony Kriz**, author, *Neighbors and Wise Men*

"I would recommend this book for all who are serious about what the church and her faithfulness in the twenty-first century can look like." **David Hillis**, president, Leadership Foundations

"A must-read book for those who are looking for creative ways to join with others in becoming a life-giving presence in your neighborhood in these uncertain times." **Christine and Tom Sine**, Mustard Seed Associates

"A gift to church leaders like me. . . . This book sets out a challenging agenda for the local church, but with such encouragement and hope that one is left in no doubt that the challenge is within reach. In fact, it's right outside our front doors." **Simon Carey Holt**, pastor, Collins Street Baptist Church, Melbourne, Australia

"A much-needed roadmap for regrounding the church in the soil of community—the key to recovering its transformative power in our urbanizing society." **Bob Lupton**, founder and president, FCS Urban Ministries

"If the missional church movement hopes to still be around for the next generation, it is going to have to keep the question of place front and center. *The New Parish* does just that while continuing to push this discussion in challenging and fruitful directions." **Eric O. Jacobsen**, author, *The Space Between*

"In contrast to a church blown by the fragmenting winds of capitalist creative destruction, consumerism and individualism, Sparks, Soerens and Friesen offer us a hopeful alternative vision." **Dan Rhodes**, editor-in-chief, *The Other Journal*

"In a society addicted to the next technique, this thought-provoking and insightful book provides a refreshing solution. God has a sense of place, and when followers of Jesus share life together and put down roots in a specific location, they become something new, something that has the power to transform and energize that community." **Felicity Dale**, author, *An Army of Ordinary People*

"In a world of increasing mobility, fragmenting relationships and a loss of any real sense of covenant, we need learn again to attend to the various people and places where God has located us. This book is a much-needed antidote to the endemic alienation of our time. Missionary grow home!" **Alan Hirsch**, author, activist, dreamer

"In stark contrast to the displacement and fragmentation that dominates our age, this important book calls us to slow down, become rooted, and experience a taste of the abundance and healing that God intends for all creation." **C. Christopher Smith**, editor, *Englewood Review of Books*

"Across North America and around the world, churches are moving into the neighborhood, faithfully rooting themselves there and connecting with neighbors to weave a fabric of care in their communities. *The New Parish* is the handbook for that movement." **John Pattison**, managing editor, *CONSPIRE Magazine*

"This book exudes the patient and passionate commitment to praxis that the authors live out in their neighborhoods. We are grateful for their collective contribution to the kingdom community." **Tom and Dee Yaccino**, Del Camino Connection

"A practical guide for any group of people committed to relevant church expressions." **Phileena Heuertz**, cofounder, Gravity: A Center for Contemplative Activism

"Full of inspiring stories and practical lessons to help Christians connect with their neighborhoods and, in the process, connect more deeply with one another and their faith." **Jim Diers**, author, *Neighbor Power*

"What a gift the notion of the parish is for our time. And what a joy to know this collective that's figuring out how to breathe life into this ancient notion." **Jonathan Wilson-Hartgrove**, author, *Strangers at My Door*

"We will be using this book as a catalyst for our own missional work and as a resource to pass on to others who are also eager to engage their neighborhoods in practical ways in the name of Christ." **Leanne and Dallas Friesen**, pastors, Mount Hamilton Baptist Church

"Paul, Tim and Dwight each live the reality they describe. I know they've paid high prices for taking a journey born out of biblical imagination and profound instincts for the practice of gospel life in North America. The path they describe is not and will not be popular. It sounds sexy and seems full of romance, but, as they well know, this is another kind of journey— without glamour, romance or individualistic heroism—focused on the agency of God and the disorienting, disturbing, disrupting work of the Spirit. We are being invited to refound the church for the sake of the healing of neighborhoods and communities in the name of Jesus. Read this book and ask how you can practice life in the 'parish.'" **Alan J. Roxburgh**, The Missional Network

PAUL SPARKS, TIM SOERENS
AND DWIGHT J. FRIESEN

THE NEW
PARISH

HOW NEIGHBORHOOD CHURCHES
ARE TRANSFORMING MISSION,
DISCIPLESHIP AND COMMUNITY

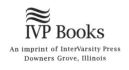
IVP Books

An imprint of InterVarsity Press
Downers Grove, Illinois

InterVarsity Press
P.O. Box 1400, Downers Grove, IL 60515-1426
World Wide Web: www.ivpress.com
Email: email@ivpress.com

InterVarsity Press® is the book-publishing division of InterVarsity Christian Fellowship/USA®, a movement of students and faculty active on campus at hundreds of universities, colleges and schools of nursing in the United States of America, and a member movement of the International Fellowship of Evangelical Students. For information about local and regional activities, write Public Relations Dept., InterVarsity Christian Fellowship/USA, 6400 Schroeder Rd., P.O. Box 7895, Madison, WI 53707-7895, or visit the IVCF website at www.intervarsity.org.

All Scripture quotations, unless otherwise indicated, are taken from THE HOLY BIBLE, NEW INTERNATIONAL VERSION®, NIV® Copyright © 1973, 1978, 1984, 2011 by Biblica, Inc.™ Used by permission. All rights reserved worldwide.

While all stories in this book are true, some names and identifying information in this book have been changed to protect the privacy of the individuals involved.

Cover design: David Fassett
Interior design: Beth Hagenberg
Images: Joe Cicak/Getty Images

ISBN 978-0-8308-4115-8 (print)
ISBN 978-0-8308-9596-0 (digital)

Printed in the United States of America ♾

Library of Congress Cataloging-in-Publication Data

Sparks, Paul, 1969-
  The new parish : how neighborhood churches are transforming mission,
  discipleship, and community / Paul Sparks, Dwight J. Friesen, and Tim
  Soerens.
      pages cm
  Includes bibliographical references.
  ISBN 978-0-8308-4115-8 (pbk. : alk. paper)
  1. Church. 2. Parishes. 3. Communities--Religious
  aspects—Christianity. 4. Fellowship—Religious aspects—Christianity.
  I. Title.
  BV600.3.S685 2014
  250—dc23
                                        2014008172

P	20	19	18	17	16	15	14	13	12	11	10	9	8	7	6	5	4	3
Y	31	30	29	28	27	26	25	24	23	22	21	20	19	18	17	16	15	14

Contents

Introduction

Three Lives Transformed by Rooting and Linking Together

When we honestly ask ourselves which persons in our lives means the most to us, we often find that it is those who, instead of giving advice, solutions, or cures, have chosen rather to share our pain and touch our wounds with a warm and tender hand.

Henri Nouwen, *Out of Solitude*

All stories have a deeper story lying just beneath the surface, and so it is with this book. This tale begins with desperation. Each of us was coming from uniquely different neighborhoods and backgrounds, but all of us were longing for colleagues who might offer friendship and encouragement. Our collective story doesn't begin with a grand vision or contagious momentum. It begins with deep hope for the church in the twenty-first century and an honest need for one another. Both of these realities remain true. Here is how, in confusion and anticipation, our stories became knit together.

FROM CONSUMER CHURCH TO THE PARISH

Paul Sparks had been pastoring a rapidly growing church. It was a GenX church born out of the early nineties Seattle grunge era. Beginning as a college-age ministry, it featured alternative worship bands and more pop culture references than you could shake a stick at. Throughout the years there were truly incredible seasons of awakening and renewal, but Paul was feeling a deep angst. There seemed to be a progressive infatuation with stage-craft and putting on a performance at the gathering. Meanwhile, there was a shrinking connection with what it meant to be the church together in the everyday realities of life.

At one point Paul took a six-month sabbatical of sorts and set out on a pilgrimage. Leaving his home, he walked sixteen hundred miles across the Pacific Northwest. He would walk for four days and then stop in a particular place to explore church ministries and neighborhoods the other three days of the week. Paul was on a quest to discover where his faith community might have gone wrong, and how the Spirit might be moving in other places. Everywhere he walked Paul discovered that when followers of Jesus were sharing life together and living in the midst of the everyday realities of a particular place, there was a vibrancy and growing maturity to their faith. Though it would be many months after Paul returned before the full implications of his experience became apparent, eventually things began to shift.

Around the turn of the century the church leadership team began moving toward deeper relational engagement and more profound connection to the cultural life of the area. Out of a deep desire to share life together and to be a living expression of the church beyond the Sunday gathering, the leadership team began calling for a move to become more deeply rooted in the heart of downtown Tacoma, Washington.

Over the months of preparation, the congregation seemed to give support to the new vision. But once the actual shifts toward parish life began to happen, the crowds that had been attending from all over the region began to shrink from hundreds to handfuls. You can imagine Paul's leadership crisis—the second guessing and the sinking feeling that he may have just made a massive mistake.

FROM ABSTRACT CONVERSATION TO REAL SHARED LIFE

Meanwhile, a few miles to the north, Dwight Friesen had recently transitioned from pastoring a network of emergent simple churches to training seminary students at The Seattle School of Theology and Psychology. As a pastor, Dwight was trying to help the congregation invest relationally together and truly know one another. But there was a persistent problem. While being known by one another was truly transformative, the geographic distance between members limited sharing life to very intentional meet-ups. Increasingly the requirement to develop relationships with each other also meant leaving the multiple contexts they felt called to serve. After eleven years, Dwight was relationally fatigued, and though the work of the academy was rigorous, he found it a welcome respite.

Dwight poured himself into his work as a professor and found his intuitive sense for seeing relational and theological connections heightened by mentors such as Dan Allender, Caprice Hollins and Stanley Grenz. His growing scholarly focus was on

forming people as followers of Christ who thought and lived out
of a deep triune ecclesiology.

But the more exciting Dwight's research on the relational
foundations of the church became, the more he felt the irony of
his growing withdrawal from meaningful shared life. He loved
the church and couldn't shake the longing to recover more holistic practices that might meaningfully weave the core facets of
church life into a more unified whole. Thus, he kept searching
for real-world examples of followers of Christ who were integrating deep community life with formative practice and meaningful engagement with their context.

FROM PROJECTS TO NEIGHBORHOOD RENEWAL

During this same time, Tim Soerens, who had pioneered a
number of missional experiments, was beginning a neigh-
borhood-based church expression in South Lake Union, in the
north part of downtown Seattle. As the months went by, Tim
found himself in a bind. On the one hand, he was invigorated
by the abundant potential for the church's engagement within
the complex dynamics of a rapidly changing urban neighborhood. On the other hand was the massive challenge of
helping a church move from coming into the neighborhood with
various projects and services, to developing a rich practice of
relational life as neighbors living together.

Tim's longing was for relational engagement in the neighborhood and a missional focus organized around holistic neighborhood renewal. Soon he found himself participating in just
about every facet of the community's life and growth. He was
asked to sit on multiple civic boards stewarding the future of the
neighborhood, and helped to build teams for a new farmer's
market, advocacy group and community center. Meanwhile, he

was inventing experiences that might draw the church into more participatory and engaging ways of living out their faith in the neighborhood together.

But the church was brand new, and very few people began in the neighborhood—and fewer still were able to move in. They hardly had time to get to know each other, let alone the neighborhood at large. Trying to play the role of community developer alone, while pastoring a group of people who hadn't really come to see themselves as members of that neighborhood, was impossible for any one person. Tim was left with a difficult burden—seeing the life and possibility the Spirit had sown all about him and feeling the pain of having very few who were able to be present long enough to see it through.

SEEDS OF HOPE

The first time the three of us were in the same room was in downtown Tacoma as Paul's church played host to a conference with Michael Frost and Alan Hirsch after the release of their groundbreaking work *The Shaping of Things to Come*.[1] We were on the lookout for some shred of support and collaboration. In most of the circles we spent time in, the parish themes we explored were like a foreign language. It was at this conference that the seeds of deep friendship and partnership were born. From that day forward, the three of us began to see how our longings and frustrations were closely aligned.

We began meeting from time to time to encourage each other, sometimes in our homes, sometimes to speak at a class, sometimes to share at our respective churches. On one occasion, Paul invited Dwight to speak words of encouragement to his now much-smaller neighborhood church. Dwight arrived about ninety minutes early just to walk the neighborhood with Paul and talk together. While this was an everyday occurrence for Paul, it was transformational for Dwight. He had never seen a pastor who seemed to know all his neighbors, much less such a diverse group. There were neighbors without homes who were trading needles out of the back of an unmarked white van, owners of the small businesses that lined the streets of downtown Tacoma, and those in intentional community at the Catholic Worker's Village living with the mentally ill, former prisoners and others without homes. Dwight felt his heart deeply stirred by the experience.

Meanwhile Tim and Paul had found another kindred spirit: a dear friend and wise pastor, Ben Katt of Awake Church in Aurora, Seattle. The friendship was generative and so encouraging. They found themselves filled with faith after they were together, daring each other to risk living even deeper into shared life within their respective communities. The more they were together the more they realized how helpful it was to have relationships with other people who were experimenting around the same themes.

Somehow this link that was forming between downtown Tacoma, South Lake Union and the Aurora Corridor enabled them to live deeper in their own neighborhoods. After talking more, sharing desires and fears and dreaming together, a few questions kept surfacing over and over. What if there were others who needed encouragement and support? After all, the three of them had felt relatively alone in their work. What if there were others who wanted to live out their faith like this in every neighborhood?

Tim, Paul and Ben began imagining what it would look like to create a relational network, a platform in which groups like their own could share encouragement, offer resources and collaborate together across places. The question that kept coming up was: *What if we intentionally tried to connect all these rooted church expressions together for mutual support both in their own parishes and across parishes?*

This question led to the founding of Parish Collective, a growing network of groups and churches that are moving toward this new parish expression. Paul and Tim began meeting with Dwight to share their excitement about the burgeoning vision. As Dwight listened he sensed the goodness of the dream and hoped that this might be a way to reconcile his personal practice with his academic life.

ROOTING AND LINKING ACROSS PARISHES

From that time forward the three of us found ourselves growing and learning together and finding as many excuses as possible to partner together. We have since traveled from neighborhood to neighborhood inviting new rooted groups to participate together in creating what we often describe as a "fabric of care" in and across parishes. Today there are hundreds of neighborhood-rooted churches and ministry expressions involved in various ways with the Parish Collective.

As these new communities were being identified it became clear they also needed to be connected. This need generated the idea of gathering parish leaders from all over the region so that others could benefit from sharing and hearing stories of living in place. The first year, Parish Collective, The Seattle School and TransFORM Network came together for what is now a celebrated annual event called the Inhabit Conference, where internationally known practitioners learn alongside local practitioners as we champion stories of local presence and renewal from around the globe.

People who were growing more involved in parish themes began asking, "Where can we get deeper training in leading our communities into the kind of imagination that permeates the conference?" Reflecting on our own stories, we decided a collaborative and immersive venue for deeper exploration could be important. After months of work, and with crucial leadership from Cathy Loerzel, vice president of advancement at The Seattle School, we began a brand new certificate program called Leadership in the New Parish.

It's been an exhilarating ride, from feeling alone to experiencing the joy that comes from friendships and the leadership of other rooted expressions. These experiences are the basis for the book you are holding now.

It would be nice to tie up all three of our stories with a nice little bow and tell you how amazing each one of our stories turned out. Although many wonderful things have happened, the truth is that the narrative of our churches and neighborhoods has been a rough ride, with ups and downs and trials and joys just like before. But here's the thing: we're still in the story.

Without the miracle of support, collaboration and guidance from the growing web of partners and practitioners experimenting in parishes, we would not have made it this far. And we are thrilled that your story might now be connected to ours in some way. We can't wait to see how God will grow the encouraging connections we've experienced together with new friends and collaborators.

HOW TO READ *THE NEW PARISH*

We wrote this book with you in mind, anticipating that you might be seeking fresh ways of following Jesus with others. As it might be imagined, we highly recommend reading it with friends and collaborators who are interested in living out their faith in everyday ways together.

As you look at the book's table of contents you will notice that the chapters are organized in response to three questions. The first question is "Why do we need a new parish?" Here we propose that the *myth of individualism* and *living above place* have fragmented the Western church. Then we chronicle the history of how the church became displaced. As you reach the end of this section we hope you will be able to name the profound fragmentation in the church and the world. But we also want you to experience an emerging sense of hope that the Spirit is on the move and the gospel offers a healing way forward.

The question framing the second section is "What is the new parish?" Here we will demonstrate just how remarkably different the new parish appears to be from the old Christendom conception. This section will begin by articulating how these new parish expressions are moving toward faithful relationship with God and with one another. Then we will locate an ecclesial life within the mutual concerns of the neighborhood. We refer to this as "the new commons."

The third section is where the rubber meets the road, focusing on the question "How do we practice the new parish?" Functioning like a field guide, the chapters in this section are filled with stories fueling your imagination for life in the neighborhood. From our many parish tours we have developed noteworthy practices that might inspire ideas for your own context.

This final section begins by offering a theory of practice in chapter six. We call this "presencing," as it creates a tangible process, enabling us to integrate the most important narratives necessary for genuine listening, authentic discernment and collective action. The seventh chapter addresses the crucial task of being rooted in a rapidly changing world, with personal and group practices that knit together an embodied fabric of caring relationships. The eighth chapter looks at how our rooted expressions in the neighborhood truly do need meaningful "linking" connections across other parishes in the city and around the world. Chapter nine reveals how the context of the parish flips our understanding of leadership upside down and helps you develop radical new ways to collaborate. The concluding chapter highlights the challenging opportunity of globalization and functions as a commissioning for you and the collaborators with whom you've been reading, discussing and experimenting.

We are grateful that you have picked up this book and are giving it a serious look. As with all writings, we know that this book is far from being the final word on the new parish. In fact, we hope it will inspire many new course-correcting conversations and experiments in the future. Please know that it is our prayer that God might use it to spark your kingdom of God imagination for the place you call home.

A FINAL WORD

We are three different people with vastly different skill sets. And while we acknowledge a book penned by three Caucasian males grossly fails to reflect the wonderful diversity of Christ's church, our similarities in no way remove our very real differences. We come from Pentecostal, Anabaptist and Reformed traditions of Christianity. We live in divergent neighborhoods and were reared in different areas of North America, even hailing from different economic classes.

In the midst of all our differences, it is important that we name the central bias we hold in common, the one that marks the pages of this book. It is our conviction that humans are meant to share life together, to learn to fit together as a living body in relationship with God, with one another, and for the place to which they are called. We think that entering into these common relationships with growing faithfulness and fidelity is what it means to be human. The gospel of Jesus enables us to live toward this full humanity. And the local church is a body that bears witness to this way of becoming human in Christ, through both manifesting that growing reality of our lives together and becoming those who see and proclaim the signs of this work happening in the people and places around us.

As audacious as this may sound, this is our hope. And so with all of our shortcomings, and with the many ways that this book will fail to capture all that God is doing in and through Christ's located church, we offer this book to you and the friends and collaborators in your church and neighborhood. May the Spirit of God be the final editor as you and your community discern the contour of faithful presence in the place you call home.

PRAYER FOR THE NEW PARISH

God of Reconciling Love,

We thank you for your reconciling mission, which is always inviting us to live in our mutual need of one another, even before we recognize it. Teach us to love and to receive one another as Christ receives us.

Amen.

Part One

WHY DO WE NEED A NEW PARISH?

1

Dislocated

Naming the Crisis We All Create

You are Christ's body. . . . You must never forget this.

The apostle Paul, 1 Corinthians 12:27 *The Message*

You think because you understand "one" you must also
understand "two," because one and one make two.
But you must also understand "and."

Ancient Sufi teaching

In August of 2000 Toshiyuki Nakagaki made a very bizarre announcement to the world. He and his colleagues had trained a type of brainless slime to solve a complex maze. To demonstrate their achievement, Nakagaki's team decided to chop up a single slime mold and scatter the pieces throughout a plastic maze. The separate slime clusters began to grow and find one another, until they filled the entire labyrinth. Next, Nakagaki placed food samples at the start and end of the maze with four different routes to the goal. Four hours later the hungry slime mold had retracted its tentacles from the dead-end corridors, growing exclusively along the shortest route between the two pieces of food. The brainless blob became "smart slime," solving the complex maze.[1]

In a world that trains you to reduce all things to the lowest common denominator, the collective characteristics of slime molds are breathtaking. When food is scarce, slimes that are in the same proximity don't fight over scarce resources. Instead, they join together in an orderly manner to form a completely new multicellular creature—a type of slug—from scratch. The right context and connectivity releases collective features you could never foresee by observing them individually.

The New Parish is an exploration of a forgotten, but truly hopeful, possibility. Don't take this the wrong way, but we think the local church is meant to function like slime.

When followers of Jesus share life together in a particular place they become much greater than the sum of their parts— they actually become something altogether new. The parish forms the context, and relationships of faith form the connectivity for wonderful new possibilities.

• • •

For several years the three of us have been connecting with churches rooted in the neighborhood. Everywhere we go, we find the Spirit working miracles of transformation through their shared life together in the parish. The consistent storyline is so encouraging. When these faith communities begin connecting together, in and for their neighborhood, they learn to depend on

God for strength to love, forgive and show grace like never before. We've also been inspired by the way these groups reach outward in love and care toward the neighborhood at large. The gospel becomes so much more tangible and compelling when the local church is actually a part of the community, connected to the struggles of the people and even the land itself.

It can be easy to miss what holds this together. By crafting a life together in a definable place, the parish becomes a platform for a whole new way of being the church. When the word *parish* is used in this book it refers to *all the relationships (including the land) where the local church lives out its faith together.* It is a unique word that recalls a geography large enough to live life together (live, work, play, etc.) and small enough to be known as a character within it.

Parish is also unique because it is a noun that holds within it a verb. It is a noun in the sense that it represents the church's everyday life and relationships within a particular place. But it also functions as an action word because it calls us to the *telos*, or purpose, of the church—living out God's dream and caring for the place we are called. Proximity in the parish allows you to participate in God's reconciling and renewing vision in ways you really can't do as an individual. We are convinced that what may seem at first like a subtle shift actually has the capacity to transform your entire experience of what it means to be the church.

THE MYTH OF INDIVIDUALISM AND LIVING ABOVE PLACE

The parish is beginning to subvert what may be the two most fragmenting forces of our day. The first can be called the "myth of the individual" and the second "living above place."

When we talk about the myth of the individual, it's not to say that people are not unique or that they do not have their own agency. It's simply to say that the individual is not autonomous. Professor Eva Feder Kittay reminds us pertly that "the independent individual is always a fictive creation of those men sufficiently privileged to shift the concern for dependence on to others."[2] All of us are born dependent on others, and whether we recognize it or not, we rely on relationships throughout our lives. "Community is the essential form of reality," writes educator Parker Palmer, "the matrix of all being."[3]

"Living above place" names the tendency to develop structures that keep cause-and-effect relationships far apart in space and time where we cannot have firsthand experience of them. For example, you have probably experienced buying groceries without any idea where the food originated or who was involved in the production and delivery process. Living above place describes the process where this type of separation happens so frequently that we become disoriented to reality.

Most people believe they have some sense of how their actions affect others. But what happens when a society lives above place for generations? Over the course of time, whole populations can develop a cocooned way of life, unaware of how their lives really affect each other and the world at large.

Your parish is a relational microcosm that helps bring many cause-and-effect relationships back together again. Being in collaborative relationships in real life (where you live, work and play) awakens you to the effects of your actions both on people and on the place itself. It creates a context where your church can see whether its faith is more than just talk. The local place becomes the testing ground, revealing whether you have learned to love each other and the larger community around you. In essence, the parish is a dare to your faith.

As more systems encourage you to create your own online

worlds and niche communities, the easier it becomes to spend time primarily with people who support your views. If people really get on your nerves you can just delete them—right? Of course, hanging out with affinity groups is not a problem in and of itself, but if you do this at the expense of practicing genuine, on-the-ground community life, serious problems can develop in nearly every dimension of life.

Social psychologist Christena Cleveland has observed that when the church left its historical focus within the neighborhood it ended up becoming homogeneous and consumer-oriented.

> Today's churchgoers . . . tend to shop for churches that express their individual values and are culturally similar. We often drive by dozens of churches en route to our church, the one that meets our cultural expectations. American society has engaged in an evangelical spiritual consumerism that some scholars pejoratively call "Burger King Christianity."[4]

Not only does living above place disconnect you from the effects of your actions, it enables you to concoct visions regarding the welfare of others without ever being in relationship with them. As Shane Claiborne, cofounder of the Simple Way community in Philadelphia, often says, it's not that we don't care about the poor. It's that we Christians don't know the poor.[5] Living above place makes it possible for you to imagine that if you just pay a tax, the government will take care of people. Or you might assume that each individual should pull themselves up by their own bootstraps and make their own way without needing others. Either way, without a practice of being with diverse neighbors in real-life contexts, it is easy to forget that humans need reciprocal friendships and communities of genuine care if they are to flourish.

Diverse neighborhoods are growing exponentially in North America, but there are still plenty of places where extreme privacy or various types of exclusion rule the day. And there are still plenty of neighborhoods where everyone looks and acts in similar ways or makes about the same amount of money. In these contexts, it is not enough to be rooted together. As this book will make clear in several ways, healthy rooting together in the local parish requires good partnering connections across parishes as well.

THE NATURE OF GOD: DYNAMIC RELATIONALITY
AND RADICAL LOCATEDNESS

Christians believe that God is revealed simultaneously as three persons in one being. The Trinity gives you an example of the paradox of individuality and community happening at the same time. This vision of uniqueness in the midst of relational unity pervades Scripture. For example, the apostle Paul gave the church in Corinth this urgent reminder regarding how they should fit together as a body:

> We all said good-bye to our partial and piecemeal lives. We each used to independently call our own shots, but then we entered into a large and integrated life in which *he* has the final say in everything. . . . The way God designed our bodies is a model for understanding our lives together as a church: every part dependent on every other part. . . . You are Christ's body—that's who you are! You must never forget this. (1 Corinthians 12 *The Message*)

If the nature of God as Trinity models your relational calling, then the incarnation of God demonstrates your missional calling to live into time and place. When God chose to enter the world, it was not in some ethereal generic manner but in a particular family, in a particular town, in a particular country with particular socio-religious practices. Just as Christ "became flesh and blood, and moved into the neighborhood" (John 1:14 *The Message*), so also the people that comprise the local church in the parish are meant to be a tangible expression of God's love in the everyday reality of life.

Shane finds it interesting that the gospel is filled with proper nouns, the names of real people and places, like Jesus of Nazareth.

> The seeds of the gospel are really small. They're really about meeting God at dinner tables and in living rooms and in little towns that may not be known by the rest of the world. But it seems like that's exactly what happens when God moves into the neighborhood in Jesus. . . . It's that which I think we're invited into is to grow into a neighborhood, to plant ourselves somewhere and to get to know people there, and to see the seeds of the kingdom grow there.[6]

When parishioners long to share relationships together, in and for a particular place, it is because they desire to reflect the nature of God in their relationships. They believe this is God's intention for what it means to be humans together in communion with the Spirit. At the end of the day, our aim is living into the fullness of life that Jesus calls us toward (John 10:10). While a relational and located perspective is at the heart of this book's understanding of what it means to be the church, it's also at the heart of what we think it means to be human.

We believe the notion of a new parish blends insights of contemporary culture, scriptural reflection and theological justification. However, being firsthand witnesses to the renewal in neighborhoods all over North America is what made our passion for these ideas take root. We've seen lives changed. We've seen communities transformed. Whole systems of brokenness and degradation have been renewed. From these real-life experiences we have become convinced that the new parish is worth our collective attention.

THE HIDDEN MOVEMENT: THE RETURN TO RELATIONALITY AND PLACE

Popular imagination holds that North American churches are dwindling away, frozen in irrelevance and dying from divisiveness. Many books on the church in recent years highlight statistics that speak of the church's decline in the Western world. While it is certainly true that all is not well within popular Christianity, those collecting the data may be asking the wrong questions. The persistent questions regarding Sunday-morning attendance, program involvement or the building budget may not be the wisest measurements for discerning the health of the church.

The new parish introduces the possibility that something spectacular is brewing beneath the level of categorical definition. Indeed, there is an immense distributed population, often unrecognized by official figures, who are learning to love their neighbors in everyday ways. Within a single mile of wherever you are reading this book, it's quite likely that there are dozens upon dozens of people who are loving their neighbor as an expression of their love of God. And here's what we find most exciting: right now there are millions more migrating toward this relational way of being the church.

Over the course of the past few years we have walked the streets, eaten in the homes, and entered the shops, gardens and ghettos of over three hundred diverse neighborhoods across North America. We have been on an expedition to discover coalescing local bodies of believers sharing life together in particular places. Throughout the course of our explorations we have stumbled on a very surprising phenomenon. Contrary to all the clamor about dying churches, the closer we get to the everyday life of people in their neighborhoods, the more we find burgeoning expressions of reconciliation and renewal.

Our dear friend Brandon Rhodes, a longtime member of the Springwater faith community in Lents, Portland, has guided us through his neighborhood, where on one strip there are five different church buildings representing five different denominations. While each church is struggling to survive and suffering from dwindling congregations, there is another story at play in the area. From simple acts of hospitality, garden sharing, urban farm harvest parties and intersection repair projects, Springwater is a tangible expression of God's love in the real life of the neighborhood. Along with neighborhood friends they have encountered along the way, members of Springwater are weaving together the fabric of love and care across the parish. Their lives bear witness to another way of living together in every dimension of life. But you would never notice this by looking at those five church buildings.

A simple switch of the imagination can produce a whole new set of questions regarding the health of the church. Here are just a few that we ask our hosts when we are visiting communities. These questions also serve as prayers as we invite God to lead our exploration. What would you ask if you were surveying neighborhoods, searching for signs of the Spirit's movement?

- Are there people who have found a way to share a life of love together here?

- Are there people leading movements toward reconciliation and renewal here?

- Are there people living on behalf of justice with the marginalized and poor here?

- Are there people entering into relational forms of civic and economic life here?

- Are there people creating reciprocal relationships of care across parishes globally here?

If we begin to ask different questions, we get different answers regarding the state of the church. What if more and more of us were on the lookout for the Spirit's movement, bearing witness to signs of new hunger for reconciled friendships, cooperative collaboration and the responsible stewardship of the place we live?

What is critical for receptivity to the new endeavor is the capacity to see how the Spirit may be at work in both the institutional church and the world at large. Both parties are finding themselves drawn from different directions toward a shared center. Throughout this text you will see a constant dialectical movement between the work of the Spirit in reforming the church and the love of God on the move in the neighborhood, drawing it toward reconciliation and renewal.

Learning to see the immeasurable and radical forces at play will require a new lens. It will require a new imagination that expands beyond our current concept of church and begins to track new patterns of renewal at work in the world. Ultimately, learning to see will require reorientation, new postures and new ways of practicing faith.

WHY IS THE WORD *PARISH* RESURFACING? WHAT'S NEW ABOUT IT?

When the three of us talk about what seems to be happening in the "new parish," it is important to distinguish from the old, or prior, understanding of parish. To propose that a new parish understanding is emerging is not to write off all that was good about the old, but to see it as the root from which new learning and growth can emerge. It also awakens us to the massive shifts in global society that mandate fresh vision and meaning for the current context.

While the ancient word *parish* carries important memories of love, home and goodness throughout its history, it also recalls various types of manipulation that have been instituted through centralized hierarchies, patriarchal structures and other forms of abuse. There have been streams of beauty and hopeful possibility, but there has also been oppression, fear and control.

We are contrasting the new parish with lingering conceptions the church has carried since Christendom, when the institutional church more or less dictated the form of the neighborhood. The church that is emerging in the parish today is different in many ways. The first difference is that the neighborhood—in all its diversity—has a voice that contributes to the form of the church. There is a growing sense that the Spirit works through the relationships of the neighborhood to teach us what love and faithfulness look like in that particular context.

The new parish is also different in the way diverse church expressions with different names and practices are learning to live out their faith together as the unified church in and among the neighborhood. Whereas the old parish was often dictated by a single denominational outlook that functioned as law, the new parish can include many expressions of the church living in community together in the neighborhood. Not only do parishioners learn to love and listen to neighbors from other church expressions in the parish, they also seek out partnerships with people from other faith perspectives who have common hopes for the neighborhood.

When we say the word *new* it does not refer to something we have invented and now present for the first time. Instead, it is a phenomenon that we have born witness to, something we have seen playing out in embryonic form that is different from the old conception. What's surprising is the origin of the *new* parish. We have found that those who have allowed the Spirit's movement in the neighborhood to give shape to the church in North America have often been urban leaders in historically under-resourced neighborhoods. These leaders are guides toward a new way of thinking about the meaning of parish.

What is both radically and profoundly hopeful is that once-disparate groups are now finding connections across places. This linking phenomenon actually changes the very nature and meaning of parish, from old typecasts of insularity and abuse to transparency, innovation and subversive ecumenism. The work that pioneers have done is catching on, spreading across parishes and coalescing toward something altogether new. It is beyond what any one of us could dream. The three of us hope to be part of those who are bearing witness to this new work and offer hopeful possibilities for the church in this new century.

PRAYER FOR THE NEW PARISH

Triune Creator,

Give us eyes to see the abundant possibility all around us. Foster within us a hunger to grow together as a loving and caring expression of Christ's body in the parish. Amen.

CONVERSATIONS FOR THE NEW PARISH

- Where do you live? Describe the contours of your neighborhood. What narratives or values seem present in the place where you live?

- What might "listening to your neighborhood" invite of you? What assumptions do you tend to make about the place you live? Why do you think you've come to believe these ideas?

- How might you describe your current relationship to your place? It may be helpful to locate yourself on the following continuum:

I live above my place

I'm a known character actively seeking the flourishing of my neighborhood

POSTURES AND PRACTICES FOR THE NEW PARISH

- **Map and marker:** Take out a map of your area and trace the outline of the definable neighborhood where you live. Mark where people live, work, play, and gather with friends and family. As you hold your place in your heart, mind and body, what are you observing?

- **Prayerful walking:** Intentionally walk your neighborhood inviting God to help you see your place with God's eyes. What signs of life, redemption, creativity, unity and love do you notice?

- **Personal story of place**: Plot out the story of your life as told through "place." How has your personal story of place shaped your relationship to place?

2

Misplaced

How the Church Lost Its Place

To be faithful to its calling,
the church must be contextual, that is,
it must be culturally relevant within a
specific setting. The church relates constantly
and dynamically both to the gospel and
to its contextual reality.

Craig Van Gelder, *Missional Church*

In 2013, rappers Jay Z and Kanye West received a Grammy for their powerful collaboration on the song "No Church in the Wild."[1] While the theology of the song is open to argument, there is little debate that the song touched a cultural nerve. Both the music video and the lyrics demonstrate that the church today is rarely found in the actual chaos of the "wild." The music video opens with a young man readying a Molotov cocktail for its target. Then, through words and images, it asserts the church is siloed in a pious prison such that it cannot engage with the everyday realities of life.

How on earth did we get to this point? How is it possible that people who follow the God who "became flesh and moved into the neighborhood" could be seen as disengaged with the real struggles of life?[2]

If chapter one offered an assessment of the crisis of the contemporary Western church living above real time and place, then this chapter will offer a reading of how the church got there. What we will see is quite striking. When local expressions of the church embrace their limitations and accept responsibility, they weave together a fabric of reconciliation and renewal. They enter back into the "wild" and discover this is exactly where the Spirit has been at work.

However, we will also see that when the church pursues power, political or economic influence, or even mission as an end in itself, its faithful presence is compromised.[3] Though it's an impossible task to do justice to the complexity of a story covering centuries, there is a common thread running through the narrative that will serve as both a cautionary tale and a story of hope. While this chapter is speaking broadly about the place-distancing trajectory of the Western church, it is vital to acknowledge that there are and have been churches in many traditions that demonstrate faithful presence within their respective neighborhoods. For example, it is worth singling out the deep commitment to place as practiced by the Jesuits for several centuries.

As we chronicle major movements of the church, be on the lookout for the ways in which the church's relationship to place changes and how that might also be reflected in contemporary reality. You will be guided by four prepositions (*in, of, for* and *with*) that describe how local faith communities in their time related to place.

THE CHURCH *IN*

Let's begin with the church of Acts after the death, resurrection and ascension of Jesus. Christ's followers are gathering in Jerusalem where they are filled with the Holy Spirit.

In those early days they began to experience what it meant to grow together as a body, after Jesus had left their physical presence. Amazing acts of love and healing were on display in their collective witness. As they "shared everything" they became a "powerful witness to the resurrection of the Master Jesus, and grace was on all of them" (Acts 4:32 *The Message*).

The church begins *in* place. In fact, the church *in* place is a dominant theme of the New Testament. Many of the letters that make up our New Testament bear witness to this. Letters are written to Jesus' followers *in* Corinth, *in* Ephesus, *in* Philippi and so on.

The word *city* meant something different in New Testament times than it does today. As the highly regarded Christian historian Rodney Stark has written, in contrast to the big cities with populations over a million like we have today, "Greco-Roman cities were small (major cities averaged under 50,000 and the places Paul traveled were often under 30,000) and extremely crowded. . . . It wasn't only lack of population that made these cities 'small'; they covered small areas and consequently were extremely dense."[4] Today such cities might be called "walkable communities."

We cannot ignore the fact that the early church was rooted in particular places. Even the few who operated as missionaries and apostles were far more connected to land, people and places than the jet-setting lifestyles of celebrity evangelists and pop religious icons today. Here Stark is worth quoting at length:

*Stark
Qr*

Paul did not rush from place to place leaving a trail of
sudden converts. Instead, he spent more than two years
building a Christian group in Ephesus, eighteen months in
Corinth, and several years in Antioch—and many histo-
rians believe his stays in some other places were consid-
erably longer than has been assumed.

Some of Paul's missionary stops did not require him to
recruit a congregation, but were visits to groups of local
Christians who already were meeting, as was the case even
in Antioch. . . . Paul did not travel alone, but often took a
retinue of as many as forty followers with him. . . . [U]pon
arrival, Paul would "gather any Christians already living in
the city," . . . and then use their social networks as a basis
for further recruitment.[5]

Synagogue as proto-parish

Prior to the Babylonian exile, Jewish worship celebrations
and congregational gatherings had been centered primarily
on the temple. But in exile, without access to their sacred
temple, the Jews needed other means of forming identity.
What emerged was the synagogue. As John M. Perkins shared
with us in an interview, "They established the synagogue . . .
within three-quarter miles of where people lived, and that
was the distance that one could go on the Sabbath day. And
so the whole idea then was to develop the neighborhood and
the community."[6]

Synagogues became the local gathering places for followers of
Yahweh within the city. They gathered for support, mutual formation, worship, storytelling and cultural preservation. Early
followers of Jesus drew on this synagogue-gathering practice,
hoping to enter the everyday life of the place and seek the peace
of the city there. Early followers of Christ gathered in synagogues
throughout the Roman Empire, but because they were increas-

ingly unwelcome within the Jewish establishment, synagogue life became difficult to maintain. As a result, churches began meeting in homes, living out Jesus' proclamation that "where two or three gather in my name, there am I with them" (Matthew 18:20).

The early church understood itself as *in* its place. This is not to say that a church was synonymous with a place; as John's Gospel shows, Jesus saw his followers as "not of the world" even as they were being "sent . . . into the world" (John 17:16, 18). Christians' primary allegiance was not to any particular vision of the economy, not to a political system or party, not even to their family, but to the reign of God practically manifested within their local context.

It was during this time that the followers of Jesus began to distinguish themselves by loving and serving their neighbors. It's amazing that in a culture much more communal than ours, the early followers of Jesus were recognized as an exceptionally loving community. In a culture defined by bloodlines and tribal identity, they excelled at welcoming strangers and even opening up to Gentiles. They became known as a people who saw dignity in all human life.

For instance, the belief in the bodily resurrection of Jesus transformed their practices around life and death. Rescuing infants from infanticide was an early practice. They also radically transformed burial rituals, as they no longer saw death as the ultimate enemy but instead as the community's opportunity to bring closure to the deceased's earthly journey with God, marked by hope in bodily resurrection.[7] This way of living in and among the people of a particular place while practicing the way of Jesus together turned out to be the necessary combination for both their own deep formation and a radical demonstration of love to the world.

THE CHURCH *OF*

The church's relationship to shared life in place radically shifted in the fourth century. Much has been written about changes in the church after the conversion of the Roman emperor Constantine. Within a few years of Constantine's conversion, the way of Jesus went from being an illegal and persecuted sect of Judaism to being the official religion of Rome. This radical change moved the center of gravity from the collective body in a particular place to the church *of* the state. *Of* is the preposition of the Christendom era.

One of the most significant shifts in church practice was the move away from localized presence to centralized power within a hierarchical church system. This shift away from being rooted *in* a particular parish had the unintended consequence of church authorities living above their place and dictating how people at the local level should behave. The technique of enforcing religious tradition and the standardization of belief forever altered the state of the church. Even the early councils—which were convened by Roman leaders rather than local churches—highlight for us the shift toward regional authority.

The irony of the effort to unify and centralize power is that it became the impetus for the most significant fractures of the church. It set the stage for an era of dueling state churches, most notably the great East-West Schism of 1054. Many factors contributed to this schism. As the Church of Rome sought to standardize power, all sorts of theological, cultural and liturgical dilemmas arose. The famous *filioque*[8] debate would eventually be the breaking point.

The power of Rome was contested as the story of the Protestant church began to unfold. People were beginning to awaken to the abuse of the state church. But, broadly speaking, the church was never able to develop a counter-imagination for more localized structures of governance. And so we witness what we might think of as the late Christendom era.

Ironically, the Protestant Reformation ended up further emphasizing the church *of*. As the nation-state was coming into being, the geo-political landscape of Western Europe was in upheaval. While individual agency grew in importance, this movement actually served to continue the trajectory of state power. To the existing Ethiopian Church, the Eastern Church and the Church of Rome were added the (Lutheran) state Church of Germany and the (Anglican/Episcopal) Church of England.

While there were exceptions, during the era of the church *of* the state, the primary energies of the church shifted away from practical love of neighbor to developing systems of belief and governance. As such, the church was disproportionately concerned with consolidating power. This prepared the way for leveraging its growing authority toward the forced missionary expansion into the new world.

THE CHURCH *FOR*

The church's story of expanding power continued with the emergence of early globalization. The modern missionary movement led the shift for expansion. The mixture of state power, missionary zeal and new trade routes to Asia led to the fairly rapid colonization of the new world—a complicated and marbled era marked by courageous women and men who were seeking to embody the good news of Christ in parts of the world that had not heard of Jesus, but also an era marked by tremendous cultural violence done in the name of Jesus.

Beginning in the sixteenth century, the Roman Catholic evangelization of the New World was linked with colonial policy.

This involved the blending of colonizing forces from Portugal, Spain and France with Roman Catholic missionaries. In fact, it was through this blending of colonial policies with the spreading of Christianity that the Portuguese were given the exclusive blessing of the pope to pursue the colonization of Asia. The papal bull (an official letter of permission from the pope) even permitted the enslavement of peoples they encountered who did not convert to Christianity—about as far removed from faithful presence as one can get.

There was little to no missionary activity from Protestants for the first hundred years after the Reformation. The Moravians launched the first large-scale Protestant missionary effort, and one of their innovations was to send lay followers of Jesus out as missionaries. But it was a Baptist cobbler named William Carey who may be most known for ushering in the modern missionary movement. In fact, he is often called the father of the modern missionary movement.

Carey's imagination for mission work had been awakened through reading about the evangelistic zeal of Jonathan Edwards, John Eliot and David Brainerd, coupled with "exotic" stories of Captain James Cook's Polynesian journeys. His primary concern was converting the "heathen," and his influence was profound. Missionary societies and denominational mission agencies began to emerge, including China Inland Mission, the Church Missionary Society for Africa, the Colonial Missionary Society and many others.

In hindsight, it's pretty obvious that abuses are inevitable when Christians come from the outside presupposing that the "heathen" needs to become just like them. When mission is seen as "over there," it's easy to mistakenly think God's dream for all people and places primarily refers to others. The Achilles' heel of missionary movements is the desire to assimilate the "other." The Western church organized its witness *for* other parts of the world and *for* unreached people groups. This desire to make others look and think like us neglects how God wants to form us collectively in the task of mission. In fact, God wants to transform all of us— perhaps especially those who are sent to faraway lands.

There is little doubt the majority of mission agencies birthed out of the church *for* had intentions to bless and serve in the name of Jesus. But we can't ignore the spiritual, physical, sexual and emotional abuses that sometimes accompanied colonial missionary work. The history of missions is complicated, and our intent is not to disparage the work of our brothers and sisters who served the sick and poor, opened hospitals, taught children to read, dug wells, started local churches and shared the good news of Jesus. Still, history shows that faithful presence can too easily be forfeited by our missionary agenda.

It is this danger that would eventually awaken a longing in the church that was *for* others to become a church *with* them.

THE CHURCH *WITH*

After Western Europe's rush to colonize the New World had run its course, the church experienced something of a relational shift. It adopted a new posture that sought to be *with*. This relational move was influenced by a number of factors, one of which was the rise of the modern evangelical movement and its emphasis on personal salvation. Compelled to see individuals make the decision to follow Jesus, modern evangelicals actually redefined the meaning of being a Christian. For the first time in the church's history a person could be a Christian *without* being a baptized member of a local congregation.

As the zeal to win converts developed, parachurch groups focused on personal evangelism and discipleship began to spring up. This meant that Christian organizations were no longer bound to the neighborhood, or even a church building, but could focus on reaching a target group. Most notably, groups like Campus Crusade, Youth for Christ and Young Life focused on building relationships with younger people in hopes of helping them order their lives around following Christ. Many evangelical churches also started to emphasize personal evangelism. Some even restructured their worship events to serve the needs of individuals who were spiritually seeking. These churches came to see personal relationships as the key to attracting new members.

Central to this relational strategy was the homogenous church-growth principle, which is built on the simple idea that people like to hang out with others who are more or less like them.[9] Churches began to market their ministries and worship services specifically to the people they viewed as their target audience, leveraging the relational networks of their members to spread the word. This made for some very large regionally based churches— a sharp contrast to the pre-war, pre-automobile era in which most followers of Christ gathered in their neighborhoods.

Jesus summed up the Old Testament Law and Prophets by saying, "Love the Lord your God" and "love your neighbor" (Matthew 22:37-39). Yet the very structure of the relational strategy that began to characterize churches drew people out of the diversity of their own neighborhood contexts; now, in a homogenous gathering, they would "consume" a worship event crafted with excellence appealing to a specific audience.

Many followers of Christ, however, did not buy into the vision of worship as a consumer event. The house church, simple church and emerging church movements sought to organize around more relational and participatory values. But without embracing the limitations of locality, the problems of homogeneity would remain. Often these movements still drew individuals according to affinity. Though it was now in a more intimate and relational setting, it still enabled members to participate without leaning into the complexity of ongoing relationships in their neighborhood.

The missional movement has since taken up the relational emphasis in a more holistic way, encouraging its members to reclaim their identity as a people of God. We have been so grateful for the missional thinkers who are inviting the church to recover its active participation in God's recreation of all things. Still, we are cautious about this. Without a recovery of place, the missional movement can end up being driven by the issue of the day. It is the mundane particularity of your place that grounds the missional impulse in the real world. Only as we seek to follow Jesus into the distinctiveness of our respective places are we invited to demonstrate our love of God by loving our neighbors.

The Church . . .

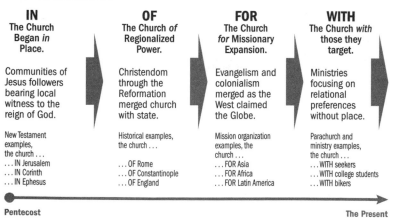

IN	OF	FOR	WITH
The Church Began *in* Place.	The Church *of* Regionalized Power.	The Church *for* Missionary Expansion.	The Church *with* those they target.
Communities of Jesus followers bearing local witness to the reign of God.	Christendom through the Reformation merged church with state.	Evangelism and colonialism merged as the West claimed the Globe.	Ministries focusing on relational preferences without place.
New Testament examples, the church . . . . . . IN Jerusalem . . . IN Corinth . . . IN Ephesus	Historical examples, the church . . . . . . OF Rome . . . OF Constantinople . . . OF England	Mission organization examples, the church . . . . . . FOR Asia . . . FOR Africa . . . FOR Latin America	Parachurch and ministry examples, the church . . . . . . WITH seekers . . . WITH college students . . . WITH bikers

Pentecost   The Present

Figure 2.1. The shifting focus of the church from Pentecost to the present

Parish ↓

GROUNDWORK FOR FAITHFUL PRESENCE IN PLACE

This brings us to our proposal for the new parish. It is simple: Follow Jesus into your neighborhood with fellow followers of Jesus. Allow the incarnation of God in Jesus Christ to form your imagination for faithful presence.

That means taking your bodies, your location and your community very seriously, as seriously as God in Christ took them. Faithful presence invites you to act on the belief that God is giving you what you need to be formed as disciples within your location.

Since prepositions have been the touchstones for this exploration of the history of the church and its relationship to place, it seems fitting to do so here as well. The exploration in the first chapter revealed both the triune and incarnational reasons for the church's presence in the neighborhood. With this in mind, the new parish movement seeks to practice *with-in place*. These two prepositions unite the *in* of the first-century church and the

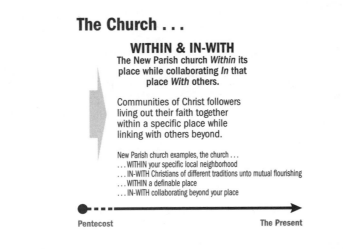

The Church . . .

WITHIN & IN-WITH
The New Parish church *Within* its place while collaborating *In* that place *With* others.

Communities of Christ followers living out their faith together within a specific place while linking with others beyond.

New Parish church examples, the church . . .
. . . WITHIN your specific local neighborhood
. . . IN-WITH Christians of different traditions unto mutual flourishing
. . . WITHIN a definable place
. . . IN-WITH collaborating beyond your place

Pentecost   The Present

Figure 2.2. The focus of the new parish

with of the missional church to ground the church in a real place. This grounding invites you to seek the flourishing of all—not just people like you, and not just people you like, but all your neighbors.

By *within* we mean standing in solidarity with your neighbors who have a shared desire to see your place be a good place to live. *Within* is about rooting within your context. You and all your neighbors desire clean air to breathe, good schools for your children, livable vocations that serve the common good, justice for all, a voice in how things are governed, and so on. You and all your neighbors want to learn and be wise, have the opportunity to grow and be healthy: physically, emotionally, spiritually, relationally. The gospel bids us to seek the flourishing of life for all.

By *within* we also mean to underscore that the only way to become faithfully present is to intentionally narrow the footprint of your life together—as was said of Jesus, who "became flesh and blood, and moved into the neighborhood" (John 1:14 *The Message*). *Within* implies that you are rooting deeply in the place God has planted you and expecting that your sense of community, your formation and your participation in God's renewing mission will integrate right where you live your everyday life.

In-with is about collaborating *in* your neighborhood *with* others unto flourishing of life for all. *In-with* may be understood as a form of missional collaboration with others who also care about your place.

Lesslie Newbigin wrote in his great book *The Gospel in a Pluralist Society*:

> The church in each place is to be the sign, instrument and foretaste of the reign of God present in Christ for that

place; a sign, planted in the midst of the present realities of the place but pointing beyond them to the future which God has promised; an instrument available for God's use in the doing of his will for that place; a foretaste—manifesting and enjoying already in the midst of the messianic tribulations a genuine foretaste of the peace and joy of God's reign.[10]

We have journeyed through the major epochs of church history and seen the complexities of each preposition. As we have observed, none of these temptations are new, and each will seduce us into living above our place. But just as Jesus was victorious over these temptations, the Spirit is longing for our victory over them—and this victory is ours in Christ. Christlike victory is not power over the other. It's not about our own success or accomplishment. And it's not about choosing our own missional identity. It's about learning a way of love together that overcomes hatred and fear and brings about healing and renewal.

Tonight, go for a walk around your neighborhood with the knowledge that God's Holy Spirit is with you. Invite God to help you see where you live, to see the people who have already been placed next to you. You need these people and they need you. Your real relationships in your neighborhood are the crucible for mutual flourishing. It is in the everyday stuff of life that love moves from the realm of spiritual ideas and becomes a costly gift, giving back more than it takes. It's in the quotidian that forgiveness and repentance cease being merely theological categories and instead become the currency of rooted relationships. The same is true of mercy, hospitality, kindness, service and the like. Your Christlike transformation is linked to the people in the place where you are.

PRAYER FOR THE NEW PARISH

God of Time and Story,

Give us the courage to listen carefully to our collective narrative as part of Christ's body that we might learn from our past what faithful presence might look like for us in our time. Help us to listen to those who have come before us with the grace and love that God offers to us. By your Spirit may the next chapter in the story reflect a hopeful new day.

Amen.

CONVERSATIONS FOR THE NEW PARISH

* As you listened to this brief telling of the church's story of place, what have you found yourself wondering about your church community's relationship to place?

* Ponder the ways in which you might need your neighbors and the ways they may need you. Is your proximity simply a coincidence? Consider writing down your thoughts to discuss with a friend, family member or parishioner in your neighborhood.

* What might be an intentional and natural next step for you to live even more fully present within and in-with your place?

POSTURES AND PRACTICES FOR THE NEW PARISH

* Research your place's history: Go to your local public library and ask a librarian to help you learn about the history of your neighborhood. Was your area home to a Native American nation? What does census data reveal? What industries have been important? What are its distinguishing geological features? What values shaped the culture of your place? What does the built environment say about your place?

- **Relate with curiosity:** As you talk with the librarian ask about his or her experience of your neighborhood. What do they love about it? What do they hope for your place? Practice curiosity and wonder as you interact with this neighbor.

- **Walk or bike:** When you go to the library consider walking or biking. Consider waving or greeting the people you encounter along the way, and try to remain open to the possibility of a conversation with a person or two as you do. Practice being interruptible.

Part Two

WHAT IS
THE NEW PARISH?

3

Faithful Presence

Ending Techniques for Renewal
That Perpetuate Fragmentation

*In Christian tradition, truth is not a concept
that "works" but an incarnation that lives.*

Parker Palmer,
To Know as We Are Known

human building

Fifty long years of drugs and prison bouts can show their signs,
but today they were barely visible. Shanice's face lit up the room.
Leaning in on the refurbished table at Firehouse Café, she
spilled the story. "My life was over . . . done . . . gone . . . finished. I was a half-white, half-black woman born here in
Richmond, Virginia. My years were filled with the pain of
racism, the addiction of drugs and that terrible ache you get
when you feel like you don't belong. But that was four years ago,
and this is now. Jesus has changed my life."

Tears were coming now, but they were tears of joy. "It's not always easy. We still have struggles. But today I own my own home, I'm running a business, I'm halfway through college, and I wake up every day caring for this neighborhood with a deep sense of purpose and identity." Shanice shared all of the things God was doing around her and finally paused for a moment of gratitude. "I give thanks every single day for what's happening here in the Highland Park neighborhood."

As she continued, it became clear that her own transformation was just the tip of the iceberg for Highland Park. The Firehouse Café where we sat was only one of many amazing start-ups of a ministry within its neighborhood called Boaz and Ruth. Founded in 2001, this organization has played a major role in transforming Highland Park from one of the most dangerous and crime-ridden areas into a bustling corridor of community life. For example, at Harvest Thrift Furniture, their flagship store and training center, more than two hundred formerly incarcerated men and women have learned and practiced the skills they need to become contributing members in their neighborhood.

By 2009 Boaz and Ruth had renovated over a dozen buildings and opened several small businesses. Their work created what they described as "a critical mass of presence" and contributed to a sixty-one percent decrease in crime. There are a number of interesting variables that make this story remarkable.

To begin with, Boaz and Ruth is in a part of town that suffers from a difficult history of racism, poverty and crime. It is located at the center of six of the seven census blocks in Richmond that had the highest number of people returning from prison. That's a tough place to get something started. On top of that, Boaz and Ruth was founded by a woman in her seventies by the name of Martha Rollins. She has no formal ministry training; she just began with what she knew: her craft of restoring furniture and her love for people. Perhaps the most surprising aspect of this story was "the plan" for getting it all started. Martha began her work by recruiting a demographic of folks who would be unlikely candidates for such an undertaking: a team of ex-prisoners who were convicted sex offenders.

In the midst of these incredible odds the cast of characters at Boaz and Ruth began trusting God, loving one another and reclaiming their parish. Today when you walk down the main street in Highland Park, you can't help but notice how it is flourishing in nearly every way. There are now multiple small businesses and outreaches, an entire block of refurbished homes, and hundreds of neighbors living renewed lives. When you see the transformation up close like this, it is pretty easy to hear the voice of God whispering, "Behold, I am making all things new."

LISTENING TO THE NEIGHBORHOOD

Shanice's story is a profound example of what is beginning to happen as people trust the Spirit together in particular places. Our work of connecting and resourcing parishes has taken us into the streets to hear these types of stories and watch the miracles taking place in hundreds of neighborhoods. While not always as dramatic, testimonies like the one in Highland Park are popping up all over North America.

Thousands of people are beginning the process of rooting in the parish and seeking a faithful way of relating together. The three of us have been, in this sense, the fortunate eyewitnesses to a movement happening beneath the radar of the larger church. And it is a turning that we believe has massive implications not only for the church in the twenty-first century, but for the lives of everyday people living in real places.

This incredible renewal is happening in large part because people like Martha Rollins and the team at Boaz and Ruth have realized that there is no controlling technique, no magic code or habits of highly effective people that can take the place of practicing love, friendship and Spirit-led collaboration within the neighborhood. In a multitude of contexts, churches, faith communities and everyday people are discovering the hope of life together in and for particular places. But you don't find this astonishing renewal by measuring numbers in the church building. You experience it in the everyday life of the parish.

We are convinced that in the midst of the pervasive brokenness the Western church is experiencing today, there are profound reasons for hope quietly unfolding in neighborhoods. But, before we can take a closer look at these seeds of renewal, we need to step back and take a sober look at how the church in North America has wound up so lost and fragmented.

As we explore the process and history of our brokenness we will find that this accelerating loss of community and disintegration of places has been happening for far too long. In fact, if we go back to the beginning of the beginning, to the Garden of Eden, we see a common refrain. Creation unfolds with the Spirit calling a people into caring relationships with a very particular place for that faithfulness to occur. But as we all know, a catastrophe occurs that continues to this day. Understanding what transpires here is crucial, for it is the ultimate poison to the flourishing of the parish.

In the primal story of the Garden we see Adam and Eve living in harmony within the parish God has placed them in. There seems to be a rich communion with the Spirit, deep friendship with each other and loving care of all the relationships within the garden. All living creatures are getting along nicely, and there are only a few instructions for the humans. The perennial favorite is "be fruitful and multiply" (Genesis 1:28 NRSV). Then there is the command to care for the land and animals. And finally, the infamous prohibition: Don't eat from the tree of the knowledge of good and evil (Genesis 2:17). But wait—there is another directive that is easy for people to miss.

With all the theological investigation the Genesis story receives, not much popular attention is given to the boundaries of the garden they are called to steward (Genesis 2:10). The Scriptures offer significant description about the location and limited size of the garden. This is rarely discussed or considered, but it is actually quite important.

We think there is a deep connection between Adam and Eve's calling to care for a specific place, and God's instructions not to eat from the tree of knowledge. After all, grasping after Godlike knowledge at the expense of relationships is a way of attempting to transcend your boundaries. It is a way of avoiding both your limitations and your responsibilities.

As we explore the garden story we see a common refrain: Creation unfolds with the Spirit calling a people into caring relationships with a very particular context for that faithfulness to occur. But a catastrophe occurs that continues to this day. Understanding what transpires here is crucial. In an age of global tools and technologies, the consequences for ignorance can be devastatingly amplified.

NAMING OUR ORIGINAL TECHNIQUE

You probably know how the story goes, but it comes across quite differently when these boundaries are kept in mind. In this "very good" creation marked by relational fidelity the serpent comes along, promising a clever technique for transcending their human limitations. "Just eat of the tree of the knowledge of good and evil, and you can have knowledge like God." Now, being like God is not a bad thing. To the contrary, one way of describing the hope of Christian discipleship is godliness. But the serpent's deception casts god-likeness as a way to bypass being truly human. Rather than living into all the limitations and responsibilities that came with their particular context, they sought to transcend it. In doing so, their relationship with their Creator was fractured.

Adam and Eve fell prey to the temptation of technique. They attempted to avoid the limits of their bodily finitude and the constraints of the place God had called them. This is how all the trouble begins, with a seduction away from true relational responsibility, and opting for a false sense of freedom. But, in the words of Elizabeth Newman, "true freedom does not lie in detachment from our created place and time (Gnosticism) nor in mastering creation (Genesis 3). Rather, freedom results from living in communion with God and others."[1] Adam and Eve made a deadly error fueled by the desire to control, and the effects of their choice grew progressively worse.

Later in the evening, when God comes calling, their strategy reverses. In the first situation they pretended to be like God, without the limitations of body and context. Now, feeling the shame of demanding transcendence, they don't even want to accept the responsibility of being human. The blame game begins, and both Adam and Eve point the finger toward others for how they have handled their agency.

In these original deceptions there is an avoidance of reality, a fleeing from the truth of what God is communicating to them through their context. On the one side they deny their bodily limitations, and on the other side they avoid their contextual responsibilities. In the end, relationships are broken (see figure 3.1).

NAMING OUR BLINDNESS

When Adam and Eve sought to transcend their limitations and to ignore their responsibilities they sacrificed faithful presence. Breaking faith with God resulted in breaking faith with each other and the created world. "Faithful presence" is a phrase that describes this relational view of the world. It means that in each situation we are listening for what our relationships require of us and responding according to our capacity. Each relationship might require a nuanced response. That is why presence is so important. We must be present to our situation, listening for what the Spirit is calling us toward. To betray that sense of calling in order to protect ourselves or control others is to be unfaithful.

Perhaps you can see glimpses of this story in your own leadership strategies. You know how it goes. It's a painful trail we've all traveled. As ministry or community leaders, we often begin strategizing for "good" outcomes. We strive for church growth, social justice or even peacemaking, but then end up doing so at the expense of faithful presence (see figure 3.1).

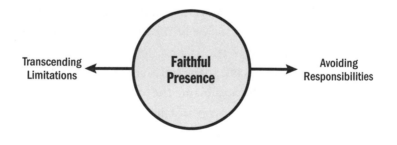

Figure 3.1. Detours from faithful presence

We get so caught up in producing outcomes through our techniques that we end up seeing everything and everyone as tools to accomplish our mission. The more reality doesn't bend to our plan, the harder we try to push our agenda. Ultimately, a sort of internal panic sets in as we begin to realize our situation is spinning out of control.

After the panic something strange often happens. Instead of admitting our brokenness and moving back toward faithful reliance on God and interdependency with one another, we tend to compound the problem. Just like Adam and Eve we blame others and refuse responsibility. It's a hopeless feeling because we imagine that others are hindering our plan for flourishing. How bizarre. We oscillate back and forth between control and hopelessness. In one moment we act as though we are transcendent like God, and in the next we deny our own human agency.

THE CYCLE OF FRAGMENTATION

This cycle of fragmentation plays out in a number of ways. For example, it happens generationally. One generation pretends to have all the answers, manipulating people at the expense of their projects. Then the next generation gives up all responsibility to act. Or consider how it often happens in politics. Each party claims they have the answers, and then they use the other party to ignore their own major blind spots. You can also see this narrative in congregations and organizations. Leaders control too much and avoid their limits. Then in response, the people take on very little and blame the leaders when things go wrong. This is an overlapping and interpenetrating cycle of avoiding limitations and responsibilities that takes place in a multitude of contexts throughout the world. But it is extremely difficult to see in oneself.

The cycle of fragmentation can often grow from generation to generation as well. In the Western world you are born into a pervasive atmosphere of technique-dependence. Before you were ever involved, it had already informed the shape of many of your cultural constructions and virtual and material environments. This makes it very difficult to see. As Catholic media theorist Marshall McLuhan showed, "Environments are invisible."[2] They are the water you swim in. They become your way of seeing the world. When that happens it is very difficult to imagine that another way is possible.

The garden narrative of avoiding limitations and responsibilities is a common deception. It runs like a constant thread throughout the Scriptures and throughout history. In a world of rapidly expanding mobility, technological power and global interconnectivity, the consequences of this cycle can have devastating effects. If all of us don't begin to name this blind spot, all of our efforts for renewal of the church in the twenty-first century will fall flat. Actually, it's probably worse than that. If our attempts at renewal do not address this cycle of fragmentation, our churches, denominations and parachurch organizations will unwittingly perpetuate the accelerating disintegration of the church today.

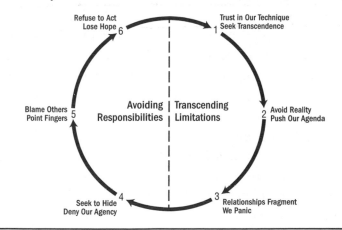

Figure 3.2. The cycle of fragmentation

TECHNIQUE AS MAGIC: EXPOSING OUR OUTCOME BIAS

While there are a variety of ways to define *technique,* in this book the three of us use the word very specifically. For us, it refers to the way many churches create standardized and uniform methods and ideologies for achieving their own desired outcomes. It is a way of creating or copying "expert strategies," believing they will work regardless of context.

When your method takes the forefront, you become distracted from what the Spirit is doing in and through your particular place. All the ways God wants to communicate through your particular situation are subverted by the narrowing logic of the technique. Slowly it ends up disconnecting you from the very means the Spirit uses to speak. Technique becomes like some sort of magic incantation that will produce results without the need for reliance on the Spirit in each context. Technique is superstition for the modern age.

There simply is no way to place your ultimate trust in the leading of the Spirit and in your expert solutions at the same time. The will to control outcomes circumvents faith in God and faithful presence toward one another. This kind of relational brokenness inevitably leads to the fragmentation of the very places churches are meant to inhabit together as God's people. The honest truth is, it's all too easy to start trusting something or someone other than God. As the prophet Bob Dylan crooned, "you're gonna have to serve somebody."[3]

Of course, it is unwise to make an overarching condemnation of strategy or abstraction in and of itself. The problem is its modern manifestation and the explosive danger that lies in the radicalization of "the idol of technique." While churches may develop programs, jobs, services, orders and so forth, the fragmentation develops when these are not subservient to real people sharing life and friendship together within a particular place and history. These best practices must always be submitted to the contextual dynamics around us and to the gift of God's grace and timing. The primary goal is not the production of outcomes, but faithful submission to the triune God and faithful action toward one another in the present.

You can see how this trap of technique can be so subtle, especially for those in ministry roles. It's not like we start the cycle of fragmentation on purpose as part of a larger plan for domination. Of course that's possible, but for the vast majority of leaders this is simply the ecosystem of ministry we are trained to maneuver. Donors want results, denominations want results, congregants want results, and conferences and books celebrate those with the requisite results.

Now, what if the vision doesn't pan out? If the vision is not achieved, the numbers don't add up, or the program doesn't get off the ground. What happens then? Well, the vast majority of us know all too well what happens. We've experienced it. Like a dam breaking, self-doubt and confusion rush into our hearts. The overwhelming feeling is one of shame, and we become like Adam and Eve when they were aware of their nakedness. We feel like we've let not only ourselves down but also the people we are working with and the people we were hoping to reach. And, most perniciously, we feel like we've disappointed God. Assessing the fallout, we often blame a scapegoat so we can cope. Or sometimes at this point we just decide to quit altogether, concluding that nothing can be done. All the while the merry-go-round of the cycle of fragmentation remains unseen.

It's so important to make this cycle visible. Author and urbanist Eric Jacobsen says that "with regard to community, it may very well be the case that what is needed is the radical intervention of a good God who is powerful enough to break the destructive cycle of sin in our lives and creative enough to weave the disparate strands of our lives into a coherent whole that we call community."[4] The task is to be honest with where you find yourself in the cycle of fragmentation and begin to place your dependence on God.

Once you see where the cycle is at work, you can start to get to the root of the problem by discerning where strategies have distorted your God-given desires. Usually this begins with your deepest longings, where you place your faith, hope and love. As humans we simply must place our faith, hope and love somewhere. The rest of this chapter will explore the ways technique distorts and ultimately misplaces these core characteristics.

MISPLACED FAITH: HUMAN TECHNIQUE OVER TRUST IN GOD'S ENDURING FAITHFULNESS

At the very core of Christianity is faith in God. How many times have we all been taught that "without faith it is impossible to please God"? To substitute faith in God for your own controlling strategies is to undermine that which is most central to the gospel. As Jacques Ellul wrote, "That which desacralizes a given reality, itself in turn becomes the new sacred reality."[5] You end up placing your faith in a false god.

In the Hebrew Scriptures there is a well-known story about the prophet Elijah entering a contest with the false prophets of the lightning god Baal. One morning both Elijah and the four hundred prophets of Baal travel to the top of Mount Carmel to build altars. There they will call out to their gods and see which one is powerful enough to consume the sacrifice for all to see. The prophets of Baal are given the first shot at the contest and begin praying to Baal. By noon, the Scriptures say, "Elijah began making fun of them."

"Pray louder!" he said. "Baal must be a god. Maybe he's day-dreaming or using the toilet or traveling somewhere. Or maybe he's asleep, and you have to wake him up." (1 Kings 18:27 CEV)

They prayed louder and louder, cutting themselves with swords and knives—a ritual common to them—until they were covered with blood. This went on until well past noon. *They used every religious trick and strategy they knew to make something happen* on the altar, but nothing happened—not so much as a whisper, not a flicker of response. (1 Kings 18:28-29 *The Message*, emphasis added).

The people were living under a systemic deception. They wanted a god that responded to the right incantation or religious technique. But Elijah's God was interested in relationship. Of course, as the story goes, when Elijah prays both the sacrifice and the altar are consumed by fire, and their worship of a false god is clearly exposed.

Perhaps we all need to ask some prophetic questions regarding our own god of technique. "Why isn't technique bringing us the life we thought it would? Surely the god of technique must be powerful. Maybe he is daydreaming or using the toilet or traveling somewhere. Or maybe he's asleep, and we have to wake him up?" It's time to stop believing the lies about technique's capacity to control the outcomes. It's time to laugh at this false god and stop paying it so much respect. It's time to return to faith in the living God.

The idolizing of human ingenuity and technological solutions permeates the Western church. Isn't it easy to devour the next how-to book? To flock to the latest leadership conference? Or to refocus your missional energies around the issues du jour?

Too often in our best efforts to serve God, love people and care for creation, it's possible to build altars to the clever. But no simple technique can guide us toward faithful Christlike presence. If we hope to experience the fullness of life that Christ promises, we have to tear the idol down.

Why is it so easy to surrender our God-given agency? Why is it so tempting to order our affections around a system of thought that another community has forged rather than operate out of the Holy Spirit's presence in our own place? Why is it so easy to believe the lie that tries to convince us that what God is doing through "them" over "there" is somehow better than what God is doing through our community here and now?

The modern Western church is addicted to the next technique. In addiction recovery work, it is often said that the first step to breaking the cycle of addiction is owning the reality of one's addiction. Technique wants your trust, even at the expense of your trust in God. It is time to own up to the addiction.

MISPLACED HOPE: PLACING CONFIDENCE IN OUR STRATEGY OVER GOD'S PLANS FOR THE FUTURE

Many in North America like to reduce the complexity of a particular situation to an abstraction. Then it can be scaled and solutions can be used in other contexts. While this can be helpful, it's so easy to forget that each context is unique. You stop being present to the actual place you're in. You lose sensitivity to what the Spirit is doing there. In the end you narrow the mystery of the relationship to something you imagine is controllable.

Any true relational process is always going to be far more complex than the schemata you devise to map it, control it or leverage it. The truth is that no map can fully replicate the whole—the map is always devised to exclude parts that do not help achieve the objectives for which it was made. For example, James C. Scott describes the designs of elite urban planners who created the original grid of most American cities. He gives a startling example of how abstracted plans and agendas can end up dehumanizing and distorting reality:

> Standardized citizens were uniform in their needs and even interchangeable. What is striking, of course, is that such subjects . . . have, for the purposes of the planning exercise, no gender, no tastes, no history, no values, no opinions or original ideas, no traditions, and no distinctive personalities to contribute to the enterprise. . . . The lack of context and particularity is not an oversight; it is the necessary first premise of any large-scale planning exercise. To the degree that the subjects can be treated as standardized units, the power of resolution in the planning exercise is enhanced.[6]

The existentialist philosopher Jean-Paul Sartre took an extreme stance on this: "Evil is the systematic substitution of the abstract for the concrete."[7] It is this *systematic* part that turns abstraction (or technique) into an evil. The three of us stand with author Mark Van Steenwyk in saying that while abstraction is necessary—even helpful at times—overreliance on abstraction is very dangerous. As Mark writes:

> Abstraction is the process in which ideas are distanced from objects. In other words, abstraction happens when we talk about the idea of people, not the concrete reality that is the person in front of you. . . . Abstraction begets evil. . . . [It] keeps us from experiencing things directly. It allows us to lose individual human beings or trees or lakes or a flower in the midst of concepts like "humanity" or "nature." By abstracting war, the nightly news makes it feel like the

same sort of thing as weather or sports. By abstracting complex realities of suffering and struggle, we can feel disconnected from those realities yet still somehow knowledgeable about them.[8]

This same phenomenon can happen in your church, organization, or denomination. You can create maps and measurements that cannot contain the true complexity of the relational process and divine mystery. In order to develop something controllable and scalable, you end up being forced to narrow what it really means to be the church together. After generations of these types of distorted and overlapping visions, the church can end up with something that barely resembles the original hope of the gospel.

This process reveals how liturgy, buildings, gatherings, services, numbers, offerings, projects, crusades, worship events and any number of religious activities and terms become separated from everyday life together in the parish. Once the definition of the church is narrowed, your hope is narrowed. Consequently, instead of longing for the flourishing of life in neighborhoods, you find yourself hoping for a diminished and individualized version of your own making.

This is not to downplay church gatherings or religious structures. It is to call attention to just how far they have become disconnected from the particulars of ordinary community life. There is an inherent simplicity to the way your church's desires can be transformed when the liturgy is directly connected to the everyday of life. Though future chapters will unpack this idea of worship as a rehearsal unto life in greater detail, you can see that gatherings are perverted and hope is exploited when they are viewed as an end in themselves.

When church is reduced to a weekly worship event, divorced from the very life God intended for humans to experience, it ends up becoming a gnostic form of spirituality. Our hope is misplaced, and we tragically aim for a distorted vision of the church achievable through strategies.

MISPLACED LOVE: CLINGING TO OUR VISION OVER LOVING PEOPLE IN THE PRESENT

Without love there is no motivation to be faithfully present to the other. Without love there is no capacity to be fully available to the Spirit's revelation. Without love there is no reason to drop your outcomes and enter into relationships with vulnerability. Love enables you to be present to the other.

It's as if the whole universe was designed for this faithful, relational presence. There's no getting around it. Jesus said that we are to abide in him, and without abiding in him we will not bear fruit. What's really interesting about this teaching from the Gospel of John is that it appears to be a strong if-then statement. If you abide in me, then you bear fruit; no abiding, no fruit. Pretty clear.

It could sound as if Jesus is offering himself as a technique for getting results. But in reality, it is just the reverse. Jesus is making technique impossible. By taking something that seems to be a static end product (production of fruit) and making it dynamic (within an ongoing relationship), technique is subverted. This is remarkable. Jesus refuses to allow us to turn him into a vending machine, even for what might appear to be good fruit.

The desire to "bear much fruit" is very good, but it can't be turned into a universal strategy. No expert can tell you how to best love your neighbor. The best experts can do is share stories of how they have loved their neighbors, or share best practices gleaned from the study of loving neighbors. Only the Spirit can guide you into faithful presence, which is the love of Christ. This is what God does.

While doing a pastoral internship years ago, Dwight was part of the church's evangelism team that followed up with first-time visitors. Though the conversations were real, there was a masterful technique behind it. Each team member memorized a carefully crafted presentation, meticulously inserting personal anecdotes at the right moments. One wintry Tuesday evening, after the process was polished, Dwight and his pastoral mentor paid a visit to a young family. It was an incredible visit. They really connected. Not only did they help the family feel welcomed, they made it all the way through the presentation. And that evening the couple decided to reorient their lives around following Christ and become active at the church. The man was so affected by the warmth of the follow-up visit that within a few months he joined the evangelism team.

Dwight can still picture the look of shock—almost betrayal—when the man learned that the team had been using a memorized evangelism strategy. He had assumed the evangelism team was just a group of caring people investing in a relationship with him. It's no fun to discover you were part of someone's scripted strategy. You feel hoodwinked.

This story highlights at least some of the complexity of relying on technique. Techniques can be efficient at producing the result they are designed for. The technique the evangelism team used was designed to produce converts, and it appeared to have worked. Yet, it's awfully tough for people to feel loved and truly known for who they are while simultaneously becoming an extension of your project.

When you trade faithful presence for techniques, people can become instrumental objects, which either aid in your mission or get in the way. Like a cookie cutter, people are pressed into your own hopes for the future. When this happens, presence—

truly being with people in the moment, with no agenda except to be faithful to what a real relationship requires—is forsaken.

Not only can technique render people as abstracted cogs in your church's missional wheel, but in the process of executing the latest strategies it ends up forming you as a people who value techniques more than being relationally present. Unwittingly, you end up engaging in a form of Christian malpractice together.

If love is not manifest concretely, toward real people and situations, it risks becoming just an ideology. It risks turning into a moral code, a sentimental notion or, worse yet, a vision that co-opts actual presence. Living this way you become malformed by the malpractice. Love that is present to the full mystery and possibility of the situation is compromised by your plans. The renowned German pastor Dietrich Bonhoeffer addressed this so clearly in the classic *Life Together*:

> He who loves his dream of a community more than the Christian community itself becomes a destroyer of the latter, even though his personal intentions may be ever so honest and earnest and sacrificial. . . . The man who fashions a visionary ideal of community demands that it be realized by God, by others, and by himself. He enters the community of Christians with his demands, sets up his own law, and judges the brethren and God Himself accordingly. . . . When things do not go his way, he calls the effort a failure. When his ideal picture is destroyed, he sees the community going to smash. So he becomes, first an accuser of his brethren, then an accuser of God, and finally the despairing accuser of himself.[9]

Actions leading to despair can be clearly seen in the growing postmodern movement of pervasive doubt in modernity and its systems of technique. In the church this plays out in multitudes of people leaving the institution altogether because of the pain and brokenness they have experienced. This may be seen in part as a result of the last two hundred years of overconfidence in the church's decontextualized conclusions about the way things are.

A RISK WORTH TAKING

The postmodern critique may be accurate—techniques are doomed to failure. But this is why you have to enter into a perpetual practice of careful responsiveness to the Holy Spirit speaking through your context. In a relationship with another person there is always the risk of doing something that doesn't help the relationship. But love never means inaction; love means listening and caring. Love means taking the risk of action; and it is a risk, for you can never know with absolute certainty what the person, or neighborhood may require.

In genuine Christian practice you don't know exactly what that transformation will look like but you enter in by faith, confident that transformation will happen. You enter into diligent practice even if the outcome is ultimately up to God. In the book *Practicing the Way of Jesus: Life Together in the Kingdom of Love,* author and activist Mark Scandrette describes this transformative mode of faithful action when he writes:

> [Jesus] invited those who were skeptical about the divine origins of his message to test the authenticity of his teaching through experiments in obedience—confident that the truth of what he taught could be proven by experience: "Anyone who chooses to do the will of God will find out whether my teaching comes from God or whether I speak on my own" (John 7:17). The way of Jesus can be verified by direct experience and must be practiced to be under-

stood. Through shared practices of obedience we can know the truth of what Jesus taught about the reality of God's kingdom.[10]

The cycle of fragmentation in the garden story will be perpetuated as long as human beings trust clever technique over a deep practice of faithful presence. God has given you the gift of limitation and responsibility. Limitations are a sign pointing to your need of the other, while responsibility reveals the other's need of you. What the physical body is to a human person, the parish is to the body of Christ. The limitation is glorious. It is God's gift enabling you to see and live into your need for others.

The three of us invite you to scour Scripture, church history and your own experience. When human beings seek after false transcendence in an effort to rise above our locatedness, evil finds a friend. Yet, when they have embodied faithful presence, strangers are loved, orphans find homes, the thirsty find water, enemies are reconciled, economies work for all one hundred percent, and the victim and perpetrator experience forgiveness.

PRAYER FOR THE NEW PARISH

Faithful, Hopeful and Loving God,

Help us to see the numerous temptations to avoid our true responsibilities and to transcend our limitations. Come to us, and form us as people who are faithfully present as Jesus Christ was faithfully present.

Amen.

CONVERSATIONS FOR THE NEW PARISH

• As you read and listened to this chapter's description of

"faithful presence," what did you hear yourself saying in response?

- As you sit with your own proclivity to transcend limitations and to avoid your true responsibilities, what practices could you intentionally deepen to become even more faithfully present? How might you reimagine the God-given limitations of your physical body and the contours of the actual place where you live as vital to becoming even more faithfully present to God, to others and in all relationships within your place?

- Tease out the implications of learning to love your place, rather than your hopes for your place. What might happen if you choose to love your place as God loves your place?

POSTURES AND PRACTICES FOR THE NEW PARISH

- **Walk with a friend or two:** Invite a neighbor to join you on your walk through your neighborhood. As you walk together share what you see and hope for.

- **Practice gratitude:** As you encounter characters who practice faithful presence, celebrate them and praise God for their lives. Practice gratitude for those things that are working in your place: sewers, gardens, schools, neighbors sharing resources, demonstrations of kindness, practices of hospitality, and so on.

- **Discern your actions:** As you are deepening your personal practice of attuning yourself to your neighborhood you will deepen awareness of some real needs, injustices and systemic forms of oppression. As you see these signs of future redemption, listen to your initial responses. What is yours to *do* and what is yours to *grieve*? (Remember that as followers of Christ we do not grieve as those without hope.)

4

Ecclesial Center

How Worship Beyond the Gathering
Reconfigures the Church

*I find that cultivating a sense of place as the exclusive
and irreplaceable setting for following Jesus is even
more difficult than persuading men and women
of the truth of the message of Jesus.*

Eugene Peterson, foreword to
Sidewalks in the Kingdom

It's Sunday morning. You're up and getting dressed while
trying to get your kids ready. After stuffing a little breakfast
into them, you pile into the car and make a sixteen-minute
drive. The family knows this is how it goes. You're a little bit
late, but frankly that's just part of the routine. After finding a
parking spot in the overflow lot, you make the trek to your
church's building. As your family enters the side door you are

greeted by one of those ultra-friendly members of the hospitality team before separating into services targeted for each age
group. The adults enter the big house (the worship audi-
torium). One child is off to join her middle school small group
near the atrium, and the youngest runs off to the kids program.
Each family member settles into a presentation carefully cu-
rated just for them. When the service concludes you meet up
again as a family at your predetermined spot—the benches
near the information desk—before heading back to your car.
Church is over until the next structured gathering.

Sound familiar? Can you at least recognize the feel of the day?
This vision of church as a service you attend on Sunday mornings
is pretty common in the Western world. Even if this isn't how it
regularly goes down in your context, you have probably experienced church like this at one time or another, or perhaps heard
about it from a friend. There's nothing wrong with going to an
event like this, but there is something wrong with thinking this
is what it means to be the church.

Imagine if your friend was trying to discern what it meant to
be a part of the church in this mode. Would they assume that it
means showing up to a weekly performance? Composing and
maintaining a shiny, happy disposition? Consuming the services of professionalized ministry? Unfortunately, this may be
all too common.

Most ministry leaders probably don't get together and say,
"What can we do to create a gathering of disconnected individuals who choose to pay for our specialized programs and
services?" Or, "We want our people to think of church as a
building, a place where our target audience goes to receive professionalized services." That would be ridiculous. Even worse
would be a scenario where the leaders intentionally planned to

*being church =
participating together
→everyday real life*

devalue people's gifts. "We want our people to get in the habit of thinking that the only important members are the ones who can sing, or preach, or give lots of money. Everyone else should just sit in the pews, look their best and give their ten percent." That would be insane.

But that's how many people end up feeling. This ends up happening because the Western world has lost one of the most important aspects of being the church: participating together as a family or body in the real-life context of the parish. Yet this is central to what it means to be the church.

LEARNING FROM CURRENT CONCEPTIONS OF CHURCH

The last chapter explained how the church ended up losing its commitment to faithful presence in the parish. But a concentrated look at how most people experience the church today, at least in Western countries, is just as crucial.

The three of us hope you will see this chapter in a hopeful light that offers new possibilities for renewing the calling of the church in the twenty-first century. Our task is not really to present a new "model" of church that competes with the multiple options that exist. For too many years even the best proposals for revitalizing the church have ended up perpetuating the endless splintering of new factions and divides. That's not what we're after.

God is up to something in neighborhoods, on the ground in real places. The church, in all its diversity, needs to figure out how to join in. We think God is putting forth a dare that, if practiced, could both revitalize church traditions, and develop a growing unity among members of various denominational expressions in the parish. More than that, it could help the church learn to give itself away in love to the world around it.

In order to explore what's possible, it's crucial to begin by naming the prevailing modes of the Western church. Learning from these conceptions will make it easier to highlight the strengths, and call forth what's missing. This is important because while each mode represents very valuable aspects of what it means to be the church, without a commitment to place they can too easily lead to the cycle of fragmentation. There are four dominant conceptions of church in the West that are important to acknowledge before exploring what is taking shape in the New Parish. Here are very brief snapshots of these common church modalities.

SNAPSHOT ONE: THE SEEKER MODE

Seeker churches have pioneered a way of organizing around felt needs. These churches take seriously how the gospel connects with the culture of the people in their region. The focus is on creating gatherings where everything relates to people who are still exploring what they believe about Jesus. It's about relating to the seekers' concerns and doing things in a way they can understand.

However, if this mode invests primary energy into gathering new people and presenting a well-crafted production, then only secondary energies are left to connect with what God is doing in the neighborhood. There is only so much organizational energy to go around. When members of a seeker church aren't real-life characters living in the neighborhood, the church tends to become oriented around the kind of consumerism we mentioned at the beginning of the chapter. It's awfully challenging to lead others to "find God in the concrete"[1] if the structure communicates that God is found and experienced only through a Sunday morning service.

SNAPSHOT TWO: THE HERITAGE MODE

The second conception of church may be referred to as the heritage mode. This mode is most often linked to a historic Christian tradition or denomination. Heritage churches invest their primary energies in passing on the beliefs, rites, rituals and core distinctives of following Christ from within their respective tradition. These churches tend to be deeply committed to the process of formation through discipleship programs or catechesis. In an age of such rapid change, the gifts of longevity coupled with a rich formative tradition are increasingly important.

The capacity to draw back from the cultural context and remember their particular story from among false competing narratives that are counter to God's desire is crucial. By telling and retelling their story it strengthens their potential to be a uniquely Christ-formed people in the world.

Most heritage churches come from traditions that took root well before the era of the automobile and began with people located in a particular place. However, things have really changed since mobility and suburban sprawl began increasing in the 1950s. Often heritage churches only have a vague recollection of when their identity was rooted in the neighborhood. This has some pretty serious consequences.

Without a dynamic living tradition shaped by the Spirit in a particular place, this once tangible expression of the church can find itself organized around static rituals. This happens largely because these traditions can be calcified into a set of denominational beliefs and liturgical practices disconnected from everyday realities. Professor Michael Warren goes so far as to say that "liturgy as aesthetics is a sham if not bonded to the loveliness of a life of struggle for fidelity."[2]

In an increasingly post-Christian culture, heritage churches are struggling to reconcile the riches of their tradition with the reality of pluralistic challenges. Having lost a deep connection to their place and culture, they are often unable to make important adaptations that growing diversity requires.

SNAPSHOT THREE: THE COMMUNITY MODE

Third is the community mode of church. The community church was the first one to realize that the modern way of life often leads to fragmentation. It was developed on the premise that what is most central for the church is deep authentic relationships with God and with one another. Community churches want to retrieve a sense of familial relationships, where each person can contribute as a meaningful participant.

This model flourished in the wake of the Jesus People movement of the late 1960s and early 1970s, and has branched out since then. Some newer expressions of the community model have gained significant traction, such as house churches, simple churches and organic churches. These kinds of groups often focus on decentralized, nonhierarchical forms of gathering that emphasize mutual participation. Some focus more on a therapeutic form of belonging, even functioning like an extended family. Others focus on a particular affinity group, bringing together people with the same struggles or of the same nationality. Churches that demonstrate deep, covenantal relationships and a mutual commitment with one another are best understood as expressions of the community mode.

While the emphasis on relationships has helped awaken the church to the need for an authentic participatory engagement, most have not recognized the importance of geographic proximity. Since this mode is not committed to life in a particular place, the only way to deepen their relationships with one another is to be drawn out of their neighborhoods to spend time together. Because those connections are a priority, it requires a tremendous investment of time outside of the places where they live.

If the community church does not have a commitment to a particular parish, it ends up violating its own relational ethos. There is simply no way for the church to develop the same kind of relationship they have with each other with those who do not belong to the church. And there is no way for the neighborhood to experience the life of the church because members live in so many places. Mission often becomes an awkward add-on to church community, because the meaning of church has not included life with people outside of their own circle of belonging.

SNAPSHOT FOUR: THE MISSIONAL MODE

The final expression to consider is the missional mode. It is the youngest of the four modes we're describing, and it grew out of a response to much of what the previous modes are missing.

The missional mode invests its primary energies in joining with God in God's mission: the practical outworking of the *missio Dei*. The doctrine of the *missio Dei* is among the most important theological developments of the last hundred years. It begins by rightly arguing that God's being and doing are one. Since God's actions always flow from who God is, so also the church should seek to unify its being and doing as one. The missional church realizes that every aspect of life should be engaged in God's redemptive plan. Mission cannot be conceived as a project of the church, rather, the church exists within God's reconciling mission.

While God's reconciling mission is central to who the church is, when this mode is separated from "life together" in a par-

ticular place, there are dangers. The first is a subtle reduction of
the church to mission. The church is more than mission, just as
God is more than mission. Think about it this way. God is love,
and mission is the loving expression of God being God. Your
longing to be a church comprised of love and faithful presence
needs to be the primary motivation for the mission of the church.

It is also important to remember that while you are created in
the image of God, you are not God. If enthusiasm to represent
God means not admitting weaknesses, you are in a serious bind.
Learning to love and forgive one another in the context of
everyday life in the community helps confront your need for
God. It keeps you humble and awake to your ongoing need for
repentance. Mission is held in tension with your own need for
the Spirit to transform your life. Popular terms like "contextual,"
"missional" and even "incarnational" can easily become "colonial."
There is not a lot of language about how we (the worshiping community) are going to be shaped and transformed by the world
around us. In order to become truly "incarnational," then we
must be reshaped by our context.[3]

If you don't have the experience of depending on God to help
you fit together as a loving body in the midst of your neighbors,
it becomes easier to arrogantly imagine that your church is going
to "take this city for Jesus." The formative and relational aspects
can be ignored. It's this reality that seems to be at the heart of
some of the darker stories of church mission that used colonizing and even violent means.

When your church's identity is reduced to mission alone you
are malformed as human beings, with a partial vision of who you
are as the church. In the mobile culture of the Western world, it
becomes possible for church expressions to do without life together in and for a particular place. By prioritizing mission over

relational life together, affinity groups will often become the target for mission. This can be contrasted with the holy motivation to know and care for the other with openness to mutuality.

In the United States especially, a blind eye cannot be turned to the history of violence toward indigenous peoples, racial oppression, manifest destiny and a contemporary impulse to act as the world's police. There is great danger in thinking that you have "the answer" for "those people" if you aren't also being formed by the Spirit's movement in that place. It is also important to be in a context where you are faced with the effects of your actions on others over the course of time.

We heartily affirm the practical and theological movement of the missional church, particularly because God's mission is obviously not limited to the walls of a church building. However, both the Scriptures and our own practice affirm the deep interdependence of our mission as the church, our receptivity to God's formative work and our relational life together. There is a tension between these dimensions of church life that hold us at the center of faithful presence. As we will see on the pages that follow, when we prioritize one of these dimensions over the others it opens the door for malformation.

These brief sketches of the prevailing modes of Western churches provide broad brush strokes for thinking about the state of the church. Of course, in practice there is a degree of overlap between all of these. These modes simply indicate how local expressions of Christ-followers are investing their primary energies.

Each of these four conceptions of church has a tendency to focus on one essential aspect of church life. The seeker mode tends to focus on the Sunday service. The heritage mode tends to focus on identity formation and preserving tradition. The community mode tends to focus on interpersonal relationships.

And finally, the missional mode tends to focus on participating with God in renewing all of creation, marked by things like social justice, peace work and evangelism. What becomes clear through this exploration is that all four modes must become present in a particular place in order to fulfill their calling faithfully.

Are we asking you to stop gathering weekly? No! Are we asking you to consider leaving the church expression you are a part of in order to join a new brand of church? No! What we are asking is that you wonder together about why you gather and about how gathering together helps you relate to one another in your everyday lives in the parish. The questions each member of a local church expression needs to ask are "How can our participation in a particular gathering grow our capacity to be a living expression of the church together in everyday life? How can it really help us to become a tangible witness of Christ's love, and to participate together in what God is doing in the place we live?"

THE ECCLESIAL CENTER: BECOMING A PEOPLE OF INTEGRATION

This section invites you to begin to reconfigure the contemporary meaning of church by incorporating the relational life within a particular place into the definition. This understanding is drawn from our discoveries in neighborhoods, reflection on the Scriptures and the practical experiences in our own contexts. The proposal takes into account the original issues we addressed in chapter two of extreme individualism and living above place. It also contributes to the renewal of each of the four modes we have just discussed. This includes being able to draw the unique contributions of each mode into a meaningful whole. We call this movement toward integration the *ecclesial center* to signify that it is the central dynamic that makes the church the church.

At the center of being the church is the worship of God. An orthodox understanding is that worship has to do with all of life. The Scriptures describe worship as "[taking] your everyday ordinary life—your sleeping, eating, going-to-work, and walking around life—and [placing] it before God as an offering" (Romans 12:1 *The Message*).

The life of worship is more than what you do together at your Sunday gathering; it encompasses the whole of your collective lives together. The worship gathering rehearses who you are and the type of people you long to be together as you live out your faith in the parish throughout the week. The local church learns to rely on the Spirit's movement in every situation as a way of being faithfully present to the relationships in your context. The holistic life of worship is an everyday posture of faithful presence. At the center of church practice is faithful presence in the parish. When the three of us use the word *worship* we are explicitly naming it as a way of life, rather than solely an event.

Christians through the ages have maintained community, formation, mission and worship as the nonnegotiable aspects of what it means to be the church. Yet we have often struggled to meaningfully hold them together. The dare of the new parish is that formation, community and mission can only be conceived of as Christian when integrated together as holistic worship; one worship life, three embodied practices. The integration of these three aspects comprises the life of holistic worship or "faithful presence." While no depiction is perfect, figure 4.1 is useful for stimulating deeper thought and practice toward an integrated understanding of the church.

- *Community* focuses on developing a common life together in the way of Christ. This includes knowing and being known by God and one another. It also means recognizing that each person has unique gifts to bring to the life of the body.

- *Formation* has to do with developing the practices and postures that shape us into mature people of faith both personally and collectively.

- *Mission* is bearing witness to the love of Jesus and the reign of God. It is joining the Spirit's movement in the neighborhood and seeking the reconciliation and renewal of all things. "The church is only the church when it exists for others."[4]

The hope is that these three elements would not simply overlap. While it's helpful to make distinctions between them, the goal is that they would increasingly grow together. The overlap represents God's vision for human flourishing.

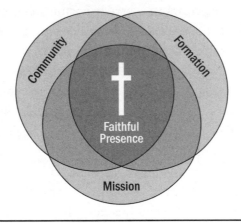

Figure 4.1. One worship life, three embodied practices

ECCLESIAL FRAGMENTATION AND THE MALFORMATION OF THE CHURCH

In an effort to be as clear as possible about the desperate need for a more integrated way of imagining the church in the everyday stuff of life, here are some exaggerated descriptions of what happens when one of these aspects is prioritized at the expense of the others.

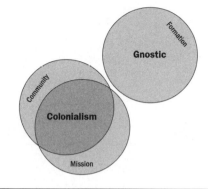

Figure 4.2. Formation separated from faithful presence

What happens if your church focuses its primary energies on formation or discipleship without developing a common life and mission together? Without the experience of sharing life together, formation is limited to teaching abstract ideas and principles and there are no examples for disciples to follow in real-life situations. Without living together with and for a particular people and place, formation loses much of its purpose.

A common mission for the reconciliation and renewal of the parish is one of the primary transformative agents: the formation of the local church. You are changed through the struggle and through your need for God's intervention on behalf of the parish. At the same time, formation is always inviting you to reassess and repent of communal practices and missional engagements that are inconsistent with God's dream.

If your church focuses primarily on its relational life together, faithful presence can be sacrificed on the altar of community. While the group members may experience a deep sense of belonging, it's altogether possible to become exclusive. On the

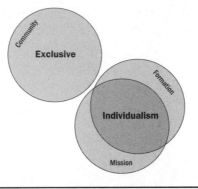

Figure 4.3. Community separated from faithful presence

other hand, without Christian community, both formation and mission may take a form of individualism (see figure 4.3). If there is no "us" to belong to, you are left with superstar Christians who might be passionate about their personal relationship with Jesus, and even could be oriented toward the well-being of others. But a collection of individuals is not the church.

Similarly, if your faith community invests their primary en-

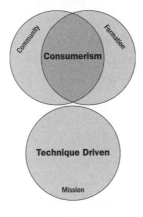

Figure 4.4. Mission separated from faithful presence

ergies in mission, they may sacrifice faithful presence on the altar of doing something for God. Many groups are engaged in peace work, evangelism, social justice or a combination of these things. But without the integration of a discerning community being formed by the narrative of the kingdom of God, the orientation of their place and their personal stories, they will become increasingly issue driven (see figure 4.4).

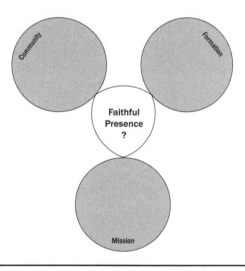

Figure 4.5. Community, mission and formation separated from faithful presence

Finally, for your church to invest its primary energies on worship events without meaningful integration of mission, formation and community would be to move toward a form of idolatry. While your church would order its gathered life in the name of Christ who gave his life for others, you would not live into this mission yourselves. Church leadership would value attendance over communal life. And because liturgy was disconnected from life, the church would end up supporting cultural accommodation more than being formed as a tangible manifestation of an alternative story. This would be a grotesque distortion of the body of Christ with only the look of a worshiping community (see figure 4.5). If this were taken to an extreme, one would have to wonder what exactly was being worshiped.

A fragmented church life creates the obvious problem of forming members of our churches as fragmented beings. But God is in the business of reconciling, not fragmenting. As the apostle Paul described the work of Christ's church he named it as the "ministry of reconciliation" (2 Corinthians 5:18). The church exists as Christ's body to form us as people who are faithfully present to God, one another and creation, even as Christ was and is faithfully present. As James K. A. Smith writes, "We are what we love."[5] Wisdom invites us to set our love on Christ and to allow that love to shape our faithful presence. When local followers of Christ engage in this process of reintegration, we find support for reconciling our whole lives within the limitations of a faith community rooted in a specific time and place. When this happens the love of God manifests itself in holistic love of neighbor.

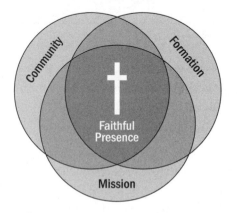

PRAYER FOR THE NEW PARISH

Triune God,

We ask that you would form our imaginations such that our hearts and minds would center on you when we think about the church. Orient our affections around your desire for our lives.

Amen.

CONVERSATIONS FOR THE NEW PARISH

- When do you most experience busyness or have a sense that the various realms of your life are more fragmented than integrated?

- The apostle Paul once defined the mission of the church as a reconciling mission (2 Corinthians 5). Engage in a thought experiment where you imagine reconciling all parts of your life. If all aspects of your life were reconciled, how would you know?

- How do you seek to embody a lifestyle of holistic worship?

- Discuss with a few friends how active involvement in the gathered practices of a church community might serve as a rehearsal for the everyday stuff of life rather than making your life busier.

POSTURES AND PRACTICES FOR THE NEW PARISH

- **Acknowledge a basic human reality:** The realms which comprise the ecclesial center (formation, community and mission as holistic worship) are basic human endeavors. All human beings worship something or someone, all are being formed, all engage in community, and all live with some kind of mission. What makes these basic human endeavors Christian is that we seek to follow Christ in these areas, properly ordering our lives as creatures in relationship with our Creator.

- **Practice of integration:** Holding this chapter's integration of formation (discipleship), community (fellowship) and mission (justice, peace making and evangelism) as holistic worship (faithful presence), begin to ask integrative questions of your personal practice. For instance, if you are engaged in a mission activity, ask, "How am I being formed as I engage in this missional task in this way? And how is community being shaped by engaging in mission in this way?" Foster an awareness of the deep integration of these realms.

- **Focus on faithful presence:** While life is full of very important things to do, the way of Christ invites us to do all that we do as an act of worship. Prioritize your practice of being present with God, others and creation. Develop little practices that help you value the relational fabric of God's creation.

5

New Commons

Finding the Church in All of Life

Our most basic common link is that we all inhabit
this small planet. We all breathe the same air.
We all cherish our children's future.
And we are all mortal.

John F. Kennedy

If you've ever been sailing, you may know that three major
components must work together to make your boat move. Naturally, you have the blowing wind that is the energy for
movement. You also have the sail that catches the wind. And
finally, you have the keel underneath the boat that links the boat
to the sea, counteracting the force of the sail. When these components come together you have motion—you're sailing.

It's all too common when talking about the church to have
Spirit-given energy (the wind) and engagement within the

church community (sail), but lack a meaningful connection to local cultural realities (the keel linking the boat to the sea). Without using the keel when you're sailing your boat is going to be set adrift. That's also what can happen when theories and programs have no connection to a local context. If the church in the parish doesn't engage the local realities of that place, then the opportunity for renewal is dead in the water.

It's worth asking: what value does the theory laid out in the previous chapter have if it cannot be practiced? Probably not much! Such a theory would be destined to float around in the vacuous realm of abstraction, and people would eventually conclude that it wasn't so meaningful after all. Any new imagination for what it means to be the church that doesn't emphasize engaging the actual world we all live in is likely to become a fad that will eventually nurture cynicism and despair. It may feel like something is happening, but in reality you wind up having some exciting conversations that never end up serving the very people for whom the church exists.[1]

This chapter will ground the previous chapter in cultural realities. You'll be able locate the ecclesial center in real time and space, enabling you to get a practical idea of what faithful presence looks like as it works its way into every dimension of life in the parish. Hopefully as you read you will remember just how good the good news is meant to be, for both you and those around you. As the church becomes faithfully present in the parish and becomes attuned to the wind of the Spirit, every dimension of life is going to be invited toward reconciliation and renewal. The three of us have seen this growing reality in hundreds of parishes around the world. So, dive into the new commons and discover an astounding opportunity for the local church of the twenty-first century to literally find itself a home.

WHAT IS THE NEW COMMONS?

Perhaps the clearest language to communicate what is meant by the word *commons* is "all that we share."[2] We add the word *new* because people share far more together than has often been acknowledged when "the commons" has been used in the past. So by *new commons* we mean all the dimensions of life for which everyone in your neighborhood shares a common concern.

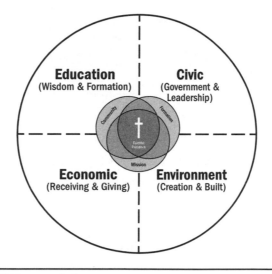

Figure 5.1. Faithful presence in the new commons

As faithful presence grows in your neighborhood, it builds healthy relationships. These relationships are critical to being human in and of themselves, but they are also the glue for engaging the commons together as community members. How people in the parish relate together around the new commons will have consequences that matter to nearly everyone. For this reason, faithful presence is at the center of the new commons. If your community cannot learn to fit together well, all aspects of the commons are destined to feel the effects.

While there may be other ways to categorize the things people share a common concern about, you may find it helpful to use the following four realms to reflect on your engagement with the commons:

- *Economy*: This includes how we collaborate together so that everyone has what they need for a flourishing life. It is a common concern because all of us desire such basic things as food and shelter.

- *Environment*: This includes all the ways we interact with the built and created world we share. At some level it is a common concern, because everyone in the parish desires clean air, good soil and a healthy place for living, working and playing together.

- *Civic*: This is about local governance and leadership. It includes the way we make decisions together in the parish. It is a common concern because all of us desire to have a say in the decisions that affect our lives.

- *Education*: This is much more than the tradition of teaching students reading, writing and arithmetic. It is about formation and wisdom, the way our context and the relationships in it end up forming people in certain ways. It is a common concern because nearly everyone desires to grow as mature and good people.

The Western world keeps people from seeing that their concerns are commonly held by focusing on them through the lens of the privatized individual. For instance, the environment is often treated as a resource of exploitation for personal or corporate gain. The civic realm is often a means of hoarding and leveraging power. The economic realm is often seen primarily in terms of personal wealth acquisition. And education is often abstracted from formation and reduced to mastery of knowledge or a set of skills deemed valuable to get a job.

But this cultural narrative is transformed by the vision of the kingdom of God that Jesus inaugurated. Followers of Christ are called to live out an alternative story of renewal in the local community. The questions you have to ask your church or group are: Do we have a redemptive way of living out these dimensions of life together as a local body? And do we have a way of engaging faithfully together with the way things currently operate in our neighborhood? Or have we narrowed down the meaning of the church to something that excludes vast segments of life?

As you reflect on each of the commons you can ask these questions as a way of discerning areas that need growth. Reflect on how you hope your faith community might function together. Then consider what small ways you could catalyze movement in that direction.

ECONOMIC: FINDING OUR FAITH IN A SPREADSHEET

Perhaps no other realm of the commons so challenges what you claim to believe than economics. Economics functions as a mirror, where the truth about your faith is reflected back. The spreadsheet is a theological statement, reflecting any incongruence between what you say you believe and how you steward your resources. This reality can be painful.

The close connection of economics to the practicing of your faith is reflected in a simple principle that Jesus communicated: "Where your treasure is, there your heart is also." Perhaps you've heard this particular saying so many times that its penetrating effect has diminished. You might think, *Right, I need to give and donate to God's purposes.* But this would be a drastic reduction of what Jesus is saying. To think of faith and economics primarily in terms of philanthropic giving is to fundamentally mistake what economics are and why they are so powerful.

At a core level economics has to do with basic exchange, receiving and giving. This exchange is behind common word pairings such as *spending* and *earning, investing* and *accruing,* or *borrowing* and *lending.* The connection between your treasure and your heart is not simply about how you give; it's also about how you earn, which means there is nothing that has to do with money that doesn't have to do with your heart. Your heart is connected to your treasure.

The ancient church developed a liturgy, still in use, called the *sursum corda* (Latin for "hearts lifted"). Here is how it's recited in thousands of churches every week:

Priest: The Lord be with you.
People: And with your spirit.
Priest: Lift up your hearts.
People: We lift them up to the Lord.

Now, imagine if you changed this liturgy by connecting our hearts and our treasure:

Priest: The Lord be with you.
People: And with your spirit.
Priest: Lift up your checkbooks, 401Ks, credit cards,
employee ID cards and the balance of all your assets.
People: We lift them up to the Lord.

Feel the difference? If you are serious about joining God in the renewal of all things, then imaginative thought and action need to go into how your church supports each other in giving and receiving, and in how you interact with the economic system at large.

The dominant version of how the economy works is no longer satisfying to the vast majority of people. For the past number of years it has become the story of unemployment, housing bubbles, the ninety-nine percent versus the one percent, the vortex of systemic greed on Wall Street that has metastasized away from being a true marketplace to resembling a virtual casino gambling on complicated bets worth billions. This is in direct contrast to the philosophy of living systems guru Pamela Wilhelms, who told us in an interview that business exists not just to increase shareholder value but "for the flourishing of life."[3]

Fortunately, there is an alternative gospel story being played out under the nose of the dominant one—a "sub-version," as Old Testament theologian Walter Brueggemann has described it. Your church or group can enter into the subversion by looking for ways to invigorate the local economy with what Peter Block and John McKnight would call an "abundant community" perspective:

- First, we see the abundance that we have—individually, as neighbors and in this place of ours.

- Second, we know that the power of what we have grows from creating new connections and relationships among and between what we have.

- Third, we know that these connections are no accident. They happen when we individually or collectively act to make the connections—they don't just happen by themselves.[4]

This is in contrast to the scarcity mindset of systems that communicate by their very nature: "You are inadequate, incompetent, problematic or broken. We will fix you. Go back to sleep."

Consider the gift economy. The gift economy most often happens with an exchange of goods and services that takes place without the medium of money. It is also the economy that's most ignored.

The gross domestic product (GDP) can be measured, but have you ever thought to measure the economic value of popping over to the neighbors' house to watch their kids for a few hours while they go to an important meeting? How about borrowing a friend's truck to haul away an old mattress? What about the millions of meals carefully prepared and then shared among friends every day? These dinners don't come with a bill after dessert.

The gift economy in your local context is crucial for economic flourishing at every level. It is all that you give and receive as a gift, an act of love, and hope and faith in relationships, that produces the kind of trust that society needs if it is to develop economies of scale. Without the social trust that develops through local gift economies, larger economies bog down with extensive rules, contracts and enforcement, or they devolve into chaos, where everyone fends for themselves.

Alvin Toffler makes an important if not humorous observation about the necessity of the gift economy. "Employers rarely recognize how much they owe to the parents of their employees. We have often made this point to corporate managers, by asking a simple, if indelicate, question: 'How productive would your workforce be if someone hadn't toilet trained it?'"[5] This "potty test" demonstrates how much larger systems of society and economy rely on the gift economy for everything they do. From the trust that the gift economy develops, other forms of giving and receiving become possible: time banks, co-ops, local currencies, gift sharing and the like.

Starting local enterprises. The imagination and perspective of the gift economy can be extended in some degree to the realm of small businesses. The three of us have found that the church has much to learn from organizations that have been doing pioneering work in the new commons for some time. Business Alliance for Local Living Economies (BALLE) is an inspiring example. Here is their stated vision for a platform that supports small businesses that contribute to local economies:

> Within a generation, we envision a global system of human-scale, interconnected local economies that function in harmony with local ecosystems to meet the basic needs of all people, support just and democratic societies, and foster joyful community life.[6]

Sounds a lot like an economy birthed out of God's vision of shalom—the kind of economic vision that followers of Jesus could get behind, right?

Local businesses may not be thought of as missional in many circles. But when you think of how BALLE talks about their reason for existence, it sounds pretty similar to holistic mission. Remember, for purposes of this book, mission is defined as what you *do* to join in God's world-renewing project. While BALLE is not faith-based, we think it's helpful to compare and contrast this type of work and what the church usually does for mission.

Local Ventures	Mission Projects
require eight hours a day and a whole-life investment	requires one to two hours a week, with a voluntary commitment
are present every day	are programmed
are intimately involved with neighbors	need to recruit others to participate
produce revenue	require donations

Figure 5.2. Local ventures versus mission projects

Of course, this chapter is not a treatise against mission projects. But it is to say that the standard definition of church mission projects is so much smaller than what is possible.

Starting and supporting any type of entrepreneurial venture in the parish is a vastly underexplored area for the church at large. You have to champion the church members who are taking risks to be present in the neighborhood.

Imagine the difference. While most ministry leaders hope members will tithe ten percent to the church, they end up with an average of about two percent. In the same way, they typically hope members will contribute ten percent of their time to the work of the church, but it's probably around two percent as well. And when it comes to contributing their real gifts, strengths and passions to the church—well, there are only a few types of "ministry" skills called for (singing, preaching and teaching being the most popular).

But if the church is *in* and *for* the parish, everything changes. While everyone may not be able to center their vocations in the parish, here are just a few ways that this shift can make a difference:

- Everything you do, everything you give, everything you buy, everything you spend time on—it all can contribute to the mission of the church and the flourishing of the parish.

- Every gift, passion and skill that contributes to the reconciliation and renewal of the neighborhood is of major value. Just *being there* can be a gift.

- Starting a small business or finding a way to live out your vocation in the parish usually helps every aspect of the commons—relationships, environment, civic life, economy, education—at the same time.

- Perhaps best of all, because you are in proximity it is easier to collaborate on these things in ways that end up making the whole far greater than the sum of the parts.

ENVIRONMENT

Brueggemann has written pointedly that "Land is a central, if not *the central* theme of biblical faith."[7] How could the land be so central a theme and yet be so neglected in contemporary understandings of what it means to be the church? All of us live in reciprocal relationship with the land. This interconnectedness means that caring for the health of your place should not be taken lightly. Restoration of the soil, the streams and all of natural creation are the gifted responsibility of the church to care for and defend. Remember, the good news of salvation extends to the reality that all of creation is healed.[8]

It's telling that some of the leading prophetic voices of the environmental movement, like Bill McKibben[9] and Wendell Berry,[10] are followers of Jesus whose faith inspires their activism. Still, there hasn't yet been a corresponding ecclesial movement. Where are the hundreds and thousands of faith communities that, because of their commitment to a particular place, are forming the infrastructure for a robust network of parishes committed to the healing of the actual land, air and water to which they call home?

The danger of having a sort of individualized environmentalism is the temptation to imagine that the problems can be solved with spectacular techniques. While all the innovation can be a helpful thing, there needs to be a shift in how people relate together and with the created world. Years ago historian Ivan Illich realized that we were not creating tools for conviviality, but ones that allowed us to remain separate from one another. "The only solution to the environmental crisis is the shared insight of people that they would be happier if they could work together and care for each other."[11]

At the end of the day the big tricks and techniques cannot

replace the slow work of learning how to relate together, localizing more of our actions, and slowing things down to human
scale so we can reflect a little more about the consequences of
decisions. We have to learn how to *be* the church again even
when the entire system of things makes it difficult to change.
Authors and parish leaders Chris Smith and John Pattison
propose that a slower church is needed.

> Slow church can help us unmask and repent of our in-
> dustrialized and McDonaldized approaches to church. It
> can also spur our imaginations with a rich vision of the
> holistic, interconnected and abundant life together to
> which God has called us in Christ Jesus. The slow food
> movement is fundamentally about the richness of a
> shared life with the neighbors who grow our food,
> prepare our food and share our food. Slow church is a
> call for intentionality, an awareness of our mutual inter-
> dependence with all people and all creation, and an at-
> tentiveness to the world around us and the work God is
> doing in our very own neighborhoods.[12]

This kind of interdependent stewardship was God's earliest
calling for humanity, and in this current age and in the age to
come you will have continued opportunities to practice living
in right relationship with the precious land God has given.

Just as God called humans to care for the land, they are also
called to steward what they make with that creation. This is referred to as the built environment. The built environment is a
powerful demonstration of our reciprocal relationship with the
created world. The ways that humans design structures end up
forming their lives and remaking them.

When you think about your neighborhood, what lifestyle was

it designed to support? For example, it's possible that you are in a suburban community with hundreds of houses, lots of roads and plenty of drive-through restaurants. This came from a particular vision of building around the convenience and mobility of car ownership. Up until the late 1950s communities were designed with other visions of life in mind.

The point is that your parish has a definite shape to it. Every building, road, park and transportation system has a formative effect. Once you become aware of this phenomenon, it can be incredibly hopeful. Even though the grid has already been laid in your neighborhood, work can be done to reshape the built environment. This is especially true if we are able to work in conjunction with businesses and municipalities for the long haul.

The literal shape of our communities is open to change if you have the vision and insight to shape them. While it may take decades to change the zoning, install new parks and gardens, and build housing for the twenty-first century, the opportunity is there if you take it. At the same time, there are thousands of smaller changes that can make a huge impact. Sometimes these acts can end up inspiring the bigger projects as well.

Consider how you have the opportunity to collaborate with the neighborhood in turning neglected spaces into cherished places. It could be an abandoned lot, an empty storefront or a neglected street.

You might think of space like this:

- Void of any true responsibility

- No story

- Meant to be passed through

Now in partnership with your community in the parish, think of how this very space could actually become a place known for:

- Shared ownership and pride

- Full of stories that elicit warm memories

- Somewhere you love to linger and invite neighbors to do the same

Doesn't this sound like meaningful work? When communities embrace the task of joining in God's renewal, it will often look like turning ignored spaces into beloved places. Brueggemann suggests that "place is indeed a protest against an unpromising pursuit of space."[13]

Not all of the attributes of place, however, can be considered unequivocally good. For some people, place is primarily associated with oppression. A place can signify the stigma of one's identity. One woman who encountered Jesus during the off hours at a watering hole understood only too well that her place carried with it certain restrictions, "for Jews do not associate with Samaritans" (John 4:9). Because a place is storied, it can evoke painful and destructive memories and can provide the pretext for relational dissociation and social stratification (thus statements like "they ought to know their place"). This underscores the need to join Jesus in the neighborhood by living into your place so that it becomes a neighborhood of mutual belonging, hospitality and openness to the other.

EDUCATION: IT REALLY DOES TAKE A VILLAGE

Tim's wife, Maria-José, is currently working on a PhD. Each year she travels with the entire family to Oxford, England, for her studies. While in England Tim gets to spend time writing and connecting with ministry leaders around the United Kingdom, but his main responsibility is caring for their three-year-old, Lukas. It can be a challenge for a little guy to acclimate to a new country, leaving behind his familiar toys, friends and routines. One dreary day, cooped up inside, Tim was near the end of his rope. The host of the home where they were staying mentioned, "You should really take Lukas to the family center a couple of blocks away. He'd love it."

Interest piqued. They quickly ventured into the rain to explore this family center with high hopes of finding Lukas somewhere to play.

As they stepped into the family center Tim's mouth dropped open, and Lukas sprinted inside as fast as possible. They discovered an entire building with toys, slides, a café, and piles of books and comfy couches. It was a dream come true for a tired dad and a rambunctious kid. After peeling off their rain gear Tim began looking for a place to pay the entrance fee. Surely this wasn't free? There are cafés like this in the United States and they cost five to ten dollars an hour for use.

Before Tim could find a checkout counter, a kind woman named Claire introduced herself. "You two are new to me. Could I get you a cup of tea?" It was all a bit too good to be true. As Tim enquired about the history of this family center, he found out local parents had been supporting this incredible place together for thirty years. And there were these types of "indoor parks" for families all over the United Kingdom. As they packed up to leave—two hours later—Tim kept thinking, *We need places like this in neighborhoods all over the United States.*

Indeed we do. It's not uncommon for church buildings to use their spaces for paid daycare. But a children's center that is led by local families and that specifically focuses on inviting young people that come from a wide range of ethnic, social, economic and cultural backgrounds is pretty unique.

As your church discerns how it joins in what God is doing in the neighborhood, it will be blessed and challenged by asking the question "How do we collectively give ourselves to the raising and educating of our youth right here?" The old adage that it takes a village to raise a child is certainly true. However, busyness, lack of neighborhood space and the bombardment of social media are rapidly changing childhood.

With this in mind, the task of the church to assist in the rearing of children has perhaps never felt so important. Raising a generation of children to become compassionate and resilient citizens in this next century is a mandate of the church, but it's not principally about creating the right program. This opportunity truly does require a village, an interlocking web of relationships. While it may be led by parents in the neighborhood, we also need single people, grandparents and college students to be contributing their gifts over the long haul.

Imagine what it would be like to grow up surrounded by dozens and dozens of aunts and uncles whom you could trust. Moreover, what if your primary understanding of what it meant to be a Christian was participating with this extended family in seeking the renewal of the neighborhood? This isn't a pipe dream. It's happening now in neighborhoods all over. But it's largely happening under the radar of the traditional church.

A dramatic and inspiring case study on this possibility is seen in the Harlem Children's Zone, a one-hundred-block community development project in Harlem. Currently led by Geoffrey Canada, the program follows children in the zone from birth to college, meshing educational, social and medical services into an interlocking web so that children are not lost to the education process due to sickness or other social challenges. "The objective is to create a safety net woven so tightly that children in the neighborhood just can't slip through."[14]

While the organizational sophistication of the Harlem Children's Zone is not something the church can necessarily replicate in every neighborhood, the concept provides a powerful vision for how generations might come together to share local wisdom that forms all residents, regardless of age.

The vision of people growing and learning as mature and good humans is not restricted to children. Education also involves the sharing of local wisdom among neighbors. Learning how to grow heirloom tomatoes from a seasoned gardener, being mentored into the craft of making a rocking chair for your front porch and the like are examples of local wisdom being shared. If you have the courage to take responsibility for the growth of the people in your neighborhood and accept a measure of responsibility for them as an extended family, it immediately changes the posture of how you interact. There are so many ways that the local culture we create contributes to how we are formed and the type of people we become.

CIVIC: LEADING AND GOVERNING IN PLACE

At its root, so much of our national political gridlock has to do with forcing ourselves to look either from a state lens or an individualistic lens when solving problems and making decisions. Of course, to gain power each side needs to demonize the other. Our friend Jim Henderson often warns, "Don't compare your best against their worst." But this has become the rule of the game for civic engagement at the national level. Moreover, this rhetorical maneuver usually happens with hot-topic issues that are divorced from real time and place. It's black or white, right or wrong, winner trying to take it all. Each side has their own media, financing and talking heads, and they are in it to win.

In such a situation, how can the church interact with the

neighborhood in a way that doesn't instantly get caught up in the classic binary between the liberal left and the conservative right? There is no magic solution for this deeply entrenched ideological battle. In the United States both the left and the right want good things. But they have a major blind spot. Daniel Kemmis, the author of *Community and the Politics of Place*, claims that the focus on individualism underlying this battle "has led us to forget this root sense of the concept of 'inhabitation.'"

> We take it for granted that the way we live in a place is a matter of individual choice (more or less constrained by bureaucratic regulations). We have largely lost the sense that our capacity to live well in a place might depend upon our ability to relate to neighbors (especially neighbors with a different life-style) on the basis of shared habits of behavior.

Kemmis goes as far as to say that "no real public life is possible except among people who are engaged in the project of inhabiting a place."[15] The church can respond to political polarization by fostering inhabitation and creating spaces to learn how to build on the things we have in common. Creating space for local civic engagement gives your community the gift of being able to say, "We made this decision, and here is what's happening now." It allows for limitation, responsibility and the capacity to see the effects of our actions.

The three of us are thankful for the dozens of national organizations seeking to reflect on the Christian narrative of God's justice and his reconciling plan for creation as it relates to niche issues coming up in Congress or Parliament. But to our limited knowledge, there are very few church-based organizations working to foster an engaging civic reality at the neighborhood level.

The future of neighborhoods and cities are often decided

around these tables in response to questions like "What new businesses are going in? How high should buildings be? What can we do to build a new park? How do we create a culture of collaboration in our neighborhood?" All of these questions and hundreds more are decided in the context of neighborhood meetings in dialogue with the broader city. It's an incredible opportunity for the church that's embedded in the neighborhood. The people who listen, advocate and work hard to knit together the good ideas being proposed need prayer and support.

The church is perhaps the only organization that is not inherently designed to be another special interest group at the table (housing, unions, business, traffic safety, developers, etc.). This is because the church is about all of life, not just "spirituality," and we should exist as connective tissue between every issue. It would be a grave mistake to think that we are present primarily to represent the interests of the church as an organization. We don't need to add another issue to the table to fight for our religious or spiritual opinions so much as we need to be listeners, integrators and relational bridge builders. If we can sit at the table as friends and neighbors, prayerfully discerning how the Spirit is asking us to build bridges, advocating for the unheard and finding creative solutions, we'll become "known as those who can fix anything, restore old ruins, rebuild and renovate, make the community livable again" (Isaiah 58:12 *The Message*).

BECOMING A COMMUNITY OF TRUST

A few years ago Tim was pioneering a new parish church in a neighborhood called South Lake Union. At the time it was the largest urban renewal project in the United States. An area that had largely been vacant parking lots, industrial warehouses and a smattering of low-income housing was being "developed" by

Microsoft cofounder Paul Allen. Mr. Allen is one of the richest people in the world. Needless to say it was a place undergoing massive change. There were new condos, apartments and millions of square feet for Amazon.com being built. Week after week Tim navigated council meetings and one-on-one meetings with stakeholders discussing the latest building proposals and architectural plans. Let's just say there were a lot of meetings.

In many ways the future of the neighborhood was being decided in these gatherings. It was in these meetings Tim began to experience a fascinating dynamic. Whether there were four people in the room or forty, it quickly became obvious to everyone precisely why they were there. One person was representing low-income housing, another trying to build a dog park, another was chiefly concerned about the building heights and so on.

What also became obvious is that no one in the room seemed to care about the neighborhood as a whole. Everyone was so focused on the outcome they were representing that a competition sometimes emerged. The question Tim found himself asking repeatedly was, "How are they going to fit together as a team for the mutual flourishing of the neighborhood?" By thinking and advocating for the whole, by meeting privately with dozens of leaders to better understand the implications of their work on the whole, it gave Tim not only a unique vantage point but also a unique authority. Quickly he became a person of trust, a person invited to the table for crucial decisions, even though he represented a small neighborhood church and had no economic clout. By showing up and advocating for holistic renewal, millions of dollars became available for low-income housing.

As we conclude this discussion of the new commons, you

might be brimming with new ideas for engagement. You also might be saying, "Hey, you three missed an important piece of the puzzle!" It's quite likely that's true. The sectors of the commons you've just read don't comprise the entirety of the local culture to be engaged by the parish church. But it's becoming clearer how the ecclesial center and the new commons can be thought of as interlocking pieces functioning within the whole of the parish. Also key at this juncture is naming just how crucial it is to become a character within the story of your parish. It's toward this task of practicing in the neighborhood that we now turn.

PRAYER FOR THE NEW PARISH

God of All People, Cultures and Places,

Your love encompasses everything in creation. By your Spirit form us into a people of holistic, inclusive love actively seeking the renewal and reconciliation of ALL people, things and places.

Amen.

CONVERSATIONS FOR THE NEW PARISH

- When you reflect on the denomination or tradition of Christianity in which you were raised or now belong, what strengths and weaknesses do you see in connecting the church to the commons?

- Reflect on the four realms of the new commons as highlighted in this chapter (environment, civic, education and economic). What might Christlike faithful presence invite in each realm within your neighborhood?

- What might happen to your identity formation if your Christian community engaged in an even more holistic vision of mission rooted in the commons?

POSTURES AND PRACTICES FOR THE NEW PARISH

- **Eyes for injustice:** Practice looking for places of injustice or inequities within the place where you live. To see an injustice and to be faithfully present within it is to have a front-row seat to God's redemptive power in the commons.

- **Kingdom of God imagination:** As you spend time in your neighborhood walking, looking, listening and talking with others who live there, develop your imagination. Dream on behalf of your place. "What if we . . . , Imagine if we . . ."

- **Eyes open for potential collaborators:** As you think about the commons, develop a posture of openness to potential partners who are already demonstrating care for your place. This can be a great opportunity to collaborate with followers of Jesus from different traditions, people from other faiths, the business sector, local government and NGOs.

Part Three

HOW DO WE PRACTICE
THE NEW PARISH?

6

Presencing

Adapting to the Spirit's Movement

*In the midst of action, you have to be able to reflect on
your own attitudes and behavior to better calibrate
your interventions into the complex dynamics
of organizations and communities.*

Ronald Heifetz, Alexander Grashow and Marty Linsky,
The Practice of Adaptive Leadership

Did you know lobsters never stop growing? The largest lobster
on record, estimated to be nearly fifty years old, weighed in at
just under forty-five pounds. What many people don't realize
is just how risky it can be to mature as a lobster. Every few
months a lobster sheds its exoskeleton. Releasing its shell is a
tiring process that leaves the flesh exposed and vulnerable. The
very creature that can look so intimidating is wide open to
attack, with no protection. Yet in order to grow, it must regu-

larly let go of that spiny, tough exterior you likely picture when you think of a lobster. Failure to rid itself of its outer shell would mean death by the very structure it previously created.

The shedding process begins when a lobster's inner being has outgrown its hardened shell. The lobster swallows large amounts of water, causing it to swell, thus pressing its flesh against the inside of its shell. Eventually this internal pressure begins to separate the carapace, which is the part of its shell protecting its head and body. Next, the lobster pops its eyes out of their holes, rending the lobster blind for the duration of the process. Then begins the slow struggle of wrenching the flesh of its large pincer claws through its much smaller joints. After the claw-flesh is free, the lobster is out with a flip of its tail. But once free, the lobster is at risk. Unable to stand for more than half an hour at a time, the lobster just flops around, tired, helpless and exposed, as it waits for its new shell to harden. If you have ever seen the cooked meat of a lobster you have likely observed the pinkish color on its outer edge. The pink is its emerging shell. The lobster's new outer structure is birthed out of what was there before. There is continuity in the transformation.

Unlike humans, lobsters appear to become more fertile with age. So even though the process of shedding its shell takes longer with age, if the lobster will continue surrendering its old structure, it will continue to produce more offspring. Lobsters mate during this time out of their shell; in fact the female *must* shed her shell, becoming more vulnerable, or her eggs cannot be fertilized.

The lobster is a metaphor for what we call "adaptive presence." How can you open up in vulnerability, shedding your old shell? What kind of courage is required to risk blindness and exposure as you move toward maturity? How can you take in the context

repentance culture

around you so that something new might emerge? How might your group become an adaptive community, able to surrender prior structures while letting your place call forth new practices?

ADAPTIVE CHALLENGES

There is little doubt that your faith community faces severe challenges in the twenty-first century. A veritable cottage industry of books, websites and events are being produced to alert the church, particularly in North America, to the reality of decline. Postcolonialism, postmodernity and post-Christian movements are just the beginning of the deep cultural forces shifting under our feet. Perhaps all that you can say with certainty is that you live in an era of uncertainty.

The complexity and confusion of this time creates what British author Ann Morisy describes as an age of chronic anxiety.[1] People desperately want the quick fix, the prepackaged solution. If you achieve some vision of success, you can bet that your story will be consolidated, copied, scaled and sold as the next thing to do. In times of change people are desperate for a new technique, but this is not what is needed.

Some might even argue that it's time to panic. After all, if you don't change you will die. Well, of course you will die if you don't change. When a body of water stops moving (constantly changing), the plants and animals living in it eventually die. Every living thing that doesn't change will die; it's a biological maxim.

The onslaught of voices pleading with the church to adapt or die is a prophetic call we must heed. But it doesn't mean we should panic or that copying others is the way forward. It means learning to truly listen and trust the Spirit's movement in our context.

When churches, denominations and seminaries face the future without clear answers for "success," the default posture can easily become protective and competitive. You look around at the shrinking numbers and think, *What can I do to just get back to what it was like in 1998?* You see all the flashy ads and sites of churches deemed "big and successful" and think, *How can we be like them? Just tell me what to do already!*

The leadership task is first one of drawing people together for mutual listening, discerning and experimenting—not fixing. If ever there was a time to experiment your way into a fresh contextual expression of the church, this is it, not only because we're living in an adaptive era but because experiments of faithful and communal presence are the best way to truly learn how to be the church in the everyday of life (see figure 6.1). You can't just think   ✱ your way there. You will have to take careful but brave steps of faith if you are going to discern your way into the future.

When the problems and answers are clear, following experts and their advice might be the way to go. But that is rarely the case in community. When facing an unknown reality that demands risk, we must tilt our attention away from the experts and toward a *community of faithful practice* that listens to their place together. As the renowned Quaker biologist Ursula Franklin says, "Work by and with mechanical citizens requires conformity, predictability, and specificity, as tasks are prescribed without reference to context. The work with and by human citizens, on the other hand, requires integration, judgment in terms of context, and interactive inventiveness."[2]

In the parish, the changing context matters. Choosing one-size-fits-all answers might be expedient, but it might not take you where the Spirit is leading. How can you and your faith community deepen your practices of listening to your place? How can you deepen your communal discernment process leading to faithful presence in your neighborhood? And how can

good Q's →

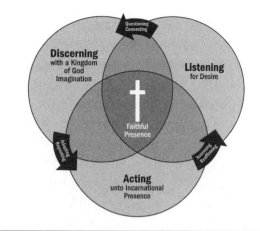

Figure 6.1. Adaptive presencing

you risk collective action that leads to the flourishing of your parish? These are the core questions propelling this chapter.

LISTENING THROUGH THE NARRATIVE BRAID

Saint Benedict of Nursia and his community developed a listening posture commonly called *lectio divina,* which is Latin for "divine reading." For Benedict, the focus of *lectio divina* was not theological analysis of biblical passages, but rather allowing the text to read you and then giving voice to what you hear the Spirit calling forth.

While Benedict and his followers primarily engaged this posture for reading Scripture, this book modifies the ancient practice to include your own story and the story of your parish. It is at the intersection of the Spirit's work through the narrative of Scripture, the story of your own life, and the needs and hopes of the people and place you live that you can begin to find wise direction for the risk of engagement. These three narrative strands woven together create an inseparable braid for adaptive presencing. In every faith community the three of us have visited where there is a robust presence in the neighborhood, these postures of the narrative braid are present.

Listening to the story of Scripture. The Scriptures offer an alternative to the technique paradigm: the gift of the Spirit, working with reconciliatory power in and through all things because of Christ. As you find yourself in the gospel narrative, you begin to confront the methodologies you have been using to circumvent faithful presence and reliance on the Spirit. Marva Dawn speaks of it as a form of tearing down idols:

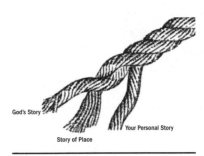

God's Story
Your Personal Story
Story of Place

Figure 6.2. The narrative braid

"One great gift of the Gospel is that it enables us to de-idolize, de-sacralize, de-divinize those elements of the technological milieu that begin unduly to take primary place in our lives and thereby fetter our hope."[3] The story of Scripture calls you back to the life of faith and communion with others, and with God's great renewing vision.

Immersing yourself in the capacious narrative of Scripture is vital if you are to listen well to your own story and the story of your place. It's a timely gift that so much of recent biblical scholarship helps all of us see Scripture as an epic story in which we can find ourselves as people. These scholars' insights are an invitation to continually discover how the biblical narrative reorganizes your imagination within an ancient but ongoing faith tradition. You come to know yourself by discovering what the Creator knows of you. A general example might be that you are created in the image of God but also as needful, dependent, desiring creatures, created in and for community.

The gospel is about the reconciliation and renewal of relation-ships. It is about God's plan through Christ to bring people who are caught in the cycle of fragmentation back into faithful rela-tionship again—with God, with one another and with the created world. The wall between us is gone. Male, female, Jew, Gentile—all our differences no longer need to divide us. When you see yourself as a character in this story, one who has been given the ministry of reconciliation to bring hope and healing to broken relationships, it can become a lens for your everyday engagement in the world.

When you read and reread Scripture, a strong case can be made that this deep desire behind God's continued action is new creation itself. In other words, "the goal of biblical history is a renewed creation: healed, redeemed, and restored."[4] This is good news! But it's also a grand universal reality with endless implications. Perhaps now you can see why listening to your story and the story of your place is so important. Quite often for the good news of God to really be digested, you need to keep listening. You must have the courage to wonder again about your own stories and the story of your place in need of healing, re-demption and restoration.

Listening to your own narrative. Anyone seeking to live faith-fully present as we are describing throughout this book will need to become a student of their own story. Daniel Taylor begins his insightful book *Tell Me a Story* by saying, "You *are* your stories. You are the product of all the stories you have heard and lived—and many that you have never heard. They have shaped how you see yourself, the world, and your place in it."[5] Yet it's easy to spend more time reflecting on what kind of car you want to buy than deeply listening to the story God is writing in and through

[handwritten margin notes: His desire mega ↳ our desire micro]

your life. Dan Allender writes, "Most people don't know how to read their life in a way that reveals their story. They miss the deeper meaning in their life, and they have little sense of how God has written their story to reveal himself and his own story."[6] Who you are, what you think and how you act within your place are all radically shaped by how you discern the multisensory social experience of your past. And in large part, you become the story you tell.

So how do you deepen your self-knowledge in the way of Christ? You must become a truth teller. Courageously lean into your story. Vulnerably share it with others who can help you hear the Spirit's calling. Ask questions of both the stories you like to recall and those stories you prefer to suppress. Together with others invite your stories to be spoken. Hear them inviting you to celebrate the joys and mourn the tragedies. Invite God to join you in the retelling of your story.

Until you wrestle with your personal narrative you will be destined to operate out of the shame of the past, compensating for abuses or perceived failings. Faithful presence is impossible if you are forever trying to cover up your addictions or the abuses you suffered at the hand of someone who was meant to love you. Any number of past stories—true or false—can lure you into living out of shame or self-condemnation. Unless you listen to your own narrative with hope in Christ, who redeems even the worst things you've ever committed, you will likely perpetuate violence (overtly or passively) even when you mean to do good.

The only way you can come to know your story well is in community with others. No one can develop true self-understanding outside of relationship. God will use the voices of every character in the neighborhood to speak to you, but special attention must be paid to those people who see themselves through the same story of Scripture. The Christian community reminds you that you are a loved child of God, that you are a full member of the body of Christ and that your primary vocation is full partnership in God's family business of reconciliation and renewal.

Listening to the narrative of your place. Listening to your place through the narrative of God's dream awakens you to what the Spirit is already up to and what good news really looks like in the place you live. There is not a program or a technique to apply. Rather, it's having an intentional posture of deep listening and openness to the reality of your place. Begin by learning to listen to what it is, not what you have assumed it to be or even what you want it to become. In a recent interview with Bill Moyers, the agrarian Wendell Berry was asked to give the answer for solving human mistreatment of the earth. His response was illuminating.

> When you ask the question "What is the big answer?" then you're implying that we can impose the answer. But that's the problem we're in to start with, we've tried to impose the answers. The answers will come not from walking up to your farm and saying, "This is what I want, and this is what I expect from you." You walk up and you say "What do you need?" And you commit yourself to say, "Alright, I'm not going to do any extensive damage here until I know what it is that you are asking of me. And this can't be hurried." . . . To be patient in an emergency is a terrible trial.[7]

[handwritten margin note: great metaphor to planting]

Listening requires trusting that while your involvement is meaningful, you are not the answer. Listening is perhaps the greatest demonstration that you do not conceive of yourself as God and that you honor others as worth listening to.

When Paul was moving into the downtown Tacoma neighborhood years ago, he and his friends did one thing right: they shut up and listened. After making so many blunders in the early stages of preparing for the transition, they knew better than to pretend to know what to do. Paul went to one of the most deeply committed and diverse faith-based nonprofits in the neighborhood, Northwest Leadership Foundation, and set up a meeting with Dave Hillis (current president of Leadership Foundations). Paul came to Dave for help, asking, "Whether it's as a volunteer or staff member, is there some way I could work here as a listener so that I don't make a mess of the work that has gone before me?" Dave, in his wisdom, brought the idea to Patricia Talton (current president of Northwest Leadership Foundation) and Annie-Jones Barnes (executive vice president), two powerful African American leaders. These two agreed to invite Paul to begin organizing and launching the City as Parish Initiative which would help inform his way of seeing the city.

While it quickly became clear that Paul wasn't a tremendous asset to his bosses, they were an incredible strength to him. For two years they taught him something new every day about the way things really work in the city of Tacoma. They didn't pull any punches in the city either. Years of work around deep issues of racism, gang violence and education issues had revealed to them the biases of a society that structures their lives in such a way as to marginalize and exclude certain groups of people without ever having to see it. Patricia made it clear: "Wisdom engages. And it benefits more than just a few. It isn't solitary. It's not private. It's for the whole."

There were a hundred ways that Paul was taking in the ethos and cultural wisdom of these two gracious leaders. Without that experience, there are so many nuances to life in the neighborhood and city Paul would not have recognized. Listening to your neighborhood involves getting to know it deeply. Here are a few questions to get you started:

- Can you walk or wheel yourself through your neighborhood on a regular basis as a prayer practice, inviting the Holy Spirit to guide you into relationships with a posture of openness?

- Have you met the local business owners within your walkable neighborhood? Who are they, how are they doing their business, and what kinds of support do they need? What about the schools? What nonprofits are present, and what do they see?

- What values shape your neighborhood's zoning laws? If your place is like many in the West, the zoning laws are often shaped by more corporate needs and automobiles than by the dignity of human life and community flourishing.

Listening to God's dream for all creation through Scripture is vital. It calls you to act faithfully in the present even as you long for the promised restoration. Listening to your own story in light of God's story helps you accept your limitations with gratitude while setting you free to take responsibility for what is uniquely yours. It is the ground for personal meaning making and vocational clarity. Listening to the story of your place opens you to the possibility of genuine relational encounter, which is mutually transformative. These three narrative strands create the ground for faithful discernment and action.

DISCERNMENT: OPENING TO THE PRESENCE OF THE HOLY SPIRIT

Discernment in the Christian tradition always takes as its starting point that God loves people, culture(s) and even the land. The goal of discernment is to spark the communal imagination toward Spirit-led action in the parish.

If Benedict of Nursia provides a path for listening, then Saint Ignatius of Loyola is a guide for discerning God's purposes for your particular place. The starting point for Ignatius and the order of Jesuits is a commitment to shared life in the parish and immersion in the story of Scripture. (Sound familiar?) When discernment is required, they begin the process by exploring personal feelings related to the issue at hand. Probing your feelings in community allows you to begin naming the real condition of your own heart and to begin nudging one another toward God's desires. Leaning into these desires together creates the opportunity to become a team of allies. As a result, you bolster each other on, encourage each other and act out of a deeper sense of how the Spirit is leading.

The Jesuit discernment process highlights four postures that members of the community live out in order to discern wisely as a collective. A person must be:

- ready to move in any direction that God wants, therefore radically free

- open to sharing all that God has given her or him, therefore radically generous

- willing to suffer if God's will requires it, therefore radically patient

- questing for union with God in prayer, therefore radically spiritual

Discernment is not about being right or wrong. It is about risking embodied engagement together with a posture of listening. As we have already mentioned, this begins with naming your emotional reaction to the decision at hand. You then discover together what you all share in common and consider what might bring flourishing in the parish itself. Failure to engage in meaningful collective discernment surrenders decisions of action to a select few and, wittingly or unwittingly, can lead to harmful decisions.

Here are a few questions to keep in your hearts and minds:

• Is the ministry of Jesus being continued in what we do?

• How might we as a gathered community be formed if we act in this way?

• Will these actions invite us to be more faithfully present to God, one another, creation and our parish?

• Will we be invited into mutually beneficial relationships with others?

• Will this action invite the flourishing of life for all and for creation?

ACTING AND THE NEW PARISH: PARTICIPATING WITH GOD IN GOD'S REDEMPTIVE MISSION

When it comes to acting according to God's redemptive mission, Saint Francis of Assisi will be the guide. Saint Francis was a person of Spirit-led action who surrendered his inherited life of wealth and privilege and identified with the poor. As Jamie Arpin-Ricci observes, "For Francis, the incarnation of Christ was the absolute act of humility and love."[8] Francis and his followers came back again and again to the simple practice of imitating the incarnational actions of Christ. He was a preacher who sought to bring good news to all God's creatures, both animals and people. Francis helped found many local communities committed to loving God by loving their neighbors.

A powerful example of this type of incarnational action, one that integrates listening and discerning, can be seen in the pioneering work of Dr. John McKnight and his colleagues. This approach to community restoration begins with the gifts and dreams already present in every neighborhood. Even the act of listening and discerning is an instrumental part of the action.

A whole mode of action has been gaining traction for the last few decades culled from their innovative model of asset-based community development (ABCD). While there are scores of books written about how asset-based development contrasts to needs-based development, the central idea is to approach transformation in our neighborhoods by identifying and connecting the dreams and assets of the people, associations and institutions that are already there.

As you seek to take action, be sure you have asked some fundamental questions: Who already lives in your parish? What do they care about? If you organize around already existing assets you usually find far greater ownership, vision and citizenship. If you concentrate on only the needs, you usually need to import professionals from outside the neighborhood.

At the heart of asset-based community development is the capacity to link your neighbors' desires, longings and skills with one another and together discern what you can do and what you already have. For years now, the three of us have been inspired by how our colleague and friend Howard Lawrence lives out this vision as a follower of Jesus in Edmonton, Canada. Only a few years ago Howard pastored what in Canada would be considered a megachurch. But Howard's life began to change when he volunteered to coach his son's soccer team in his beloved neighborhood called the Highlands. He couldn't believe how many parents and kids were literally right next to him that he missed as a busy pastor seeking to care for a large regional congregation. The dissonance between the integration he experienced in the Highlands and the frenetic activity of trying to care for a congregation that was spread out all over the region eventually led him to focus solely on his neighborhood. It was a significant change, and one he's grateful he made.

Howard is now constantly interacting with his neighbors, teasing out their hopes and ideas for how the Highlands can become an even more vibrant and connected place. The momentum has grown so powerfully that the city of Edmonton is working with Howard to create an "Abundant Communities Initiative,"[9] mobilizing neighborhood organizers to knock on as many doors as possible to build "a culture of connection."[10] The success of this initiative has generated quite a bit of interest in Howard's neighborhood, in other neighborhoods of Edmonton, and also with local newspapers and television stations.

What's remarkable is that Howard's active presence in the neighborhood is simultaneously highly strategic and deceptively simple. He and his neighbors are knitting together a movement of relational care, not only through their individual work but also by encouraging and mobilizing other neighbors to act and curate collaborations in the neighborhood.

Taking inspiration from Howard's experience in the Highlands, think about action in your parish. Consider these practical ideas:

- Find out what people love about the neighborhood, and nurture that affection.

- Ask your neighbors about one thing they wish existed in the neighborhood. Then ask if they would be willing to help make it happen if they had help.

- Convene neighbors with common gifts and desires and ask one another what could be accomplished together.

The process of listening, discerning and acting is never really finished. Nor is it always so cyclical. It's not as if there is a starting line where you can check off the listening box and forget about it. Still, you and your community will likely find seasons in which one of these postures is especially crucial.

This adaptive presencing process is an integrative one that brings the postures of listening, discerning and acting together with one goal: faithful presence in your neighborhood. When all three facets are attended to within a community, the individual members function as a local expression of the family of God and are active participants in God's family business, the renewal of all things.

PRAYER FOR THE NEW PARISH

God, grant us the wisdom to listen attentively to your presence all around us. May we listen well to your dream for creation. May we listen well to our own lives. And may we listen well to the people and the place we call home. By your Spirit enable us to discern our calling and have the courage to act.

Amen.

CONVERSATIONS FOR THE NEW PARISH

- Review the three strands of the narrative braid (the redemptive plot of God's story, the contextual setting of your place and the character of your personal story); what story might God be writing in you and in your place?

- Discuss the process of adaptive presencing (listening, discerning, acting). Which of these three is your group's strength? Which could be developed more? What small steps might you attempt in order to graciously invite meaningful experimentation?

- Explore what can happen when groups of Christians jump to action without deep listening and collective discernment.

POSTURES AND PRACTICES FOR THE NEW PARISH

- **Community of discernment:** Consider what practices could be developed within your faith community that could form you to be even more intentional about collectively discerning what the Holy Spirit is inviting. What is the hope and reason for your gatherings?

- **Ongoing cycle of presencing:** The presencing cycle of listening, discerning and acting is an ongoing process. Once your group has listened carefully and discerned a course of action, continue listening. As you act you often discover unintended consequences or discover that you may have missed an important stakeholder in your process. What are you learning about yourselves through this process?

- **Loving without agenda:** Often our neighborhoods are filled with special interest groups. The church is not a special interest group; rather we have a reconciling mission that seeks unity, that all might flourish. Consider how your faith community can champion what others are already doing.

7

Rooting

Growing Stability Within Your Place

*To be rooted is perhaps the most important and
least recognized need of the human soul.*

Simone Weil, *The Need for Roots*

There are no meanings apart from roots.

**Walter Brueggemann,
*The Land: Place as Gift, Promise,
and Challenge in the Biblical Faith***

The metaphor of rooting obviously comes from plant life.
Plants sink roots deep into the ground to connect to the nu-
trients necessary for thriving while simultaneously anchoring
themselves against life's occasional storms. The psalmist uses
this same rooting metaphor to contrast the wise with the foolish.
The wise—deeply rooted in God's dream of renewal—are a

stable presence producing fruit and shade for those around
them, while the foolish are fragmented and scattered like chaff
by even the slightest breeze (Psalm 1). The rooting of people
within a parish is similar.

Rooting is, to use Jonathan Wilson-Hartgrove's language,
about "staying put and paying attention."[1] It is coming to know
your neighborhood and becoming one of its characters. It is
teasing out with curiosity the story of your place.

- Who are the characters who gave it form?

- What are the forgotten tragedies?

- Who knows and tells this history?

Rooting within the parish is about coming to love your neighborhood—your whole neighborhood. Dr. Cornel West often says
that you can't lead the people unless you love the people. Ex-
tending this contemporary proverb is true for your place as well.
It happens as you open up and let your place teach you about its
shape, geography, history, peoples, cultures and so on. As you
come to know it you will see your need of it, and its need for you.
You will come to love the place you share. In his poetic wisdom
Wendell Berry sums this up by saying: "It all turns on affection."[2]

BEGINNING WITH YOU: ROOTING AS A PERSONAL PRACTICE

Most people are longing for a more integrated and connected
life. Followers of Jesus want to be the church together in
deeper ways than simply attending professionalized church
programs. But when you are in the middle of a broken system
it is hard to see your everyday life through the prism of God's
imagination. The economic structures, the built environment
and the cultural value system are not oriented around this
sharing of life. The only way to get started is to begin by

adapting some of your everyday practices with a posture of prayerful possibility.

Personal practices are simply the routines, patterns and everyday habits you carry out in the neighborhood that give you the opportunity to engage with what's happening. In a very real sense, this is about your public presence in the parish. Most of *local* your presence in the neighborhood is incredibly ordinary, but *habits* that doesn't mean it shouldn't be *intentional*. For example, you decide to drink coffee at the local café instead of driving miles away. You play pickup basketball with neighbors at the park around the corner instead of playing in a church league. You and a few neighbors decide to share a meal every Wednesday, or you pick a time to meet each week at the playground where the kids can play together.

You might be thinking to yourself, *Is this your brilliant idea for joining God in the renewal of all things? To drink coffee at the local café?* Of course none of these practices appears to be earth shaking, but they will always be the starting place for weaving together a fabric of care and for illuminating what's possible. And sometimes really big changes occur as a result of ordinary personal practices.

Our friend Majora Carter has a pretty impressive résumé. She's won multimillion dollar grants for neighborhood renewal. She's been awarded a MacArthur Genius Award. She's earned a Peabody Award for a radio program on local change-makers. And she gave one of the most famous TED talks, with luminaries like Al Gore in the front row. What some folks might not know is that her activism and entrepreneurial career began with a simple personal practice: jogging with her dog in the neighborhood.

One morning Majora was out for a run, passing the all-too-common dumpsites peppered across the South Bronx in New York City. On this fateful day her dog wouldn't stop pulling her toward the Bronx River. Since there was no access, she had to gingerly walk past weeds and piles of garbage. As her dog strained forward through the dilapidated landscape, she passed a massive city dump site that ended abruptly near the shore of the river. The refuse of the city—the garbage from the wealthy neighborhoods on the other side of town—had been dumped in front of one of her neighborhood's most valuable natural assets. In that moment she experienced awakening. Her neighborhood was worth fighting for, and fight she did.

While Majora's discovery of the neglected riverbank in her neighborhood was an accident, this epiphany became a catalyst in what has become a prolific career of activism, environmental restoration and local entrepreneurialism. Today a beautiful river-front park has been built by the community because Majora was jogging with her dog, stumbled upon a discovery and took responsibility for her neighborhood.

As Majora reminds everyone who will listen, "You don't have to move out of your neighborhood to live in a better one." But it begins with you. Developing your personal practice of rooting can open the door to wonderful possibilities.

ROOTING TOGETHER AS A FAITH COMMUNITY

It's absolutely crucial to start developing your personal practice. The old wisdom that "you can't take people where you haven't traveled yourself" is certainly true in the transition toward a more rooted and stable life. However, until there is a faith community to be seen, a web of relations integrating their lives, a viable church in the parish will always remain an ideal. Jon Tyson, founding pastor of Trinity Grace Church in New York

City, paints a compelling picture of how rooting together as a church community within a common proximity could tangibly demonstrate everyday acts of love:

> What would the Church look like if we chose to buy homes in the same streets and subdivisions, the same buildings and blocks, the same suburbs and sections? What would our love look like if it showed up dozens of times a week in small but profound ways: meals cooked, prayers prayed, songs sung, Scripture studied, games played, parties thrown, tears shed, reconciliation practiced, resources given? What if we stopped attending community groups and became groups of communities? What if our homes stopped being the places we hid from the world but havens to which the world comes for healing?[3]

Each of us finds ourselves in different life stages and scenarios. To adopt this new perspective is not about being a certain kind of person; it's about being you, with your friends, in your neighborhood and integrating your day-to-day routines within your unique place. That being said, because the structure of Western life has become so fragmented, it may seem that your situation is impossible and that you don't even know where to begin. Here are a few of the most common situations. Where do you find yourself? Use the following categories and questions to help discern what next steps might bring more integration for you and your church community.

Where do you see yourself?

Outside-in. You don't currently live in the parish where your faith community meets and is active, yet you are committed to what that community is about and want to contribute at a deeper level.

- Is it possible to move to that neighborhood?

- Can you realign other activities of your life into that parish to increase the likelihood of doing life together?

Inside-out. You don't currently live in the parish where your faith community meets and is active, but your faith community encourages you to collaborate with your neighbors to join in God's renewal efforts where you do live.

- Ask your neighbors, "How could we partner together for beauty and renewal in this neighborhood we share?"

- Ask God to lead you into relationships with other people who follow Christ in your neighborhood and step into the places where people intersect and meet one another.

- Keep an open and prayerful heart as you carefully discern the place you are called to inhabit. Remember, it's not about arrival, it's about prayerful hope and faithful action.

With-in. You worship in the same parish you live in, and you are open to collaborating with other Christians.

- How can you adapt your personal practices to make even more connections with other Christians in the parish, regardless of where they attend worship gatherings?

With-out. For various reasons you haven't found a faith community in your parish, but you want to connect with other Christians where you can join in God's renewal right where you are.

- Continue to pray for partners as you live out your personal practice in the neighborhood.

- Reach out to wider networks like the Parish Collective (www .parishcollective.org) to find potential new partners.

- Write a paragraph on the importance of gathering. Write a paragraph on championing the small.

ROOTING WITH OTHER PEOPLE OF FAITH IN THE NEIGHBORHOOD

One of the ironies of life in the mobile world of consumer church is that it's possible to miss people who love God that are living right in your neighborhood. But once your group establishes the practices needed to fit together as an expression of the local church within the parish, you will find yourselves confronted with an important question: How do we view those followers of Christ who may be from other church expressions but are members of the same parish—perhaps even our next-door neighbors? Surely God must look at all the people trusting the Spirit in the neighborhood that are from different denominations and traditions and say, "That's my church."

Sound confusing? Admittedly, it's a pretty foreign concept. But whereas you might think of yourself as belonging to a church plant of twelve people, with a parish imagination, the number of people in your church might be five hundred, or even five thousand. That's an awfully big church (unless, of course, you're in Texas). While diverse church expressions, gatherings and affiliations may be important, or even critical within the parish, it doesn't mean that you shouldn't find ways to entangle your daily life in collaboration together as the whole body of Christ in the neighborhood. Every church is more properly understood to be a part of the church in their particular neighborhood. In your unity together, so much more is possible.

Paul was doing some parish organizing in Vancouver, Canada, when he encountered the downtown Eastside neighborhood corridor for the first time. On a tour with Jonathan Livingston from Alongsiders International he discovered something beautiful that rarely happens. In what is known as the one of most difficult places in Vancouver, there were over ten intentional communities and a number of other ministries representing the whole bandwidth of denominational difference. In the midst of all their differences, they had found a way of working together in various ways on behalf of the neighborhood. Each of these groups had their own ethos, practices and gatherings, but in many ways they were collaborating and connecting as one church. Shocking! Astonishing! Beautiful!

Entering into the beauty of this possibility means that in just about everything, you need to have humility. Whether you are a pastor, business owner, nonprofit leader, artist or whatever, you share your gifts and callings as part of the team in the neighborhood. The root of the word "collaboration" stems from the Latin *com-* ("with") and *laboro* ("work"). Your capacity and imagination grow exponentially when you look at everything in your parish through a "with" lens. Suddenly, the suffering you see in your neighborhood is shared. The gifts are shared. The responsibility is shared. Joyously, the celebration of God's acting in and through the parish is shared. Truly, when we begin to see what's possible through a "with" lens, the future of the church is not so dark after all. There is a veritable megachurch in just about every neighborhood in North America, if only you have the eyes to see.

ROOTING WITH PEOPLE FROM OTHER TRADITIONS AND FAITHS

Tony Kriz is a master storyteller who can spin a hundred yarns, each more amazing than the next. Whether it's around the dinner table or speaking at a college or writing in a book, you can bet he is going to shift your imagination about the way of Jesus. But it was a serious eye-opener when Tony released a book filled with stories about how the Spirit used people that Tony saw as "religious outsiders" to awaken his faith and reveal God's genuine love and goodness. Even more surprising were the countless stories Tony shared from the Gospels, where Jesus reveals religious outsiders demonstrating great faith or genuine goodness to awaken the insiders.

The last chapter of his book *Neighbors and Wisemen* (which refers to the religious outsider stories of the good Samaritan and the Magi who came with gifts at Jesus' birth) contains these words:

> In my life, more often than I have wanted to admit, the themes of God's story have come from people who did not wear my same religious uniform, did not have my same spiritual name badge (Hello! My religion is . . .), and certainly did not come from my same background or experiences. But they were God's voice all the same. . . . The *other* person is not my enemy. They are the hands of my healing and the mouthpiece of my enlightenment.[4]

Once you believe that the Spirit is at play in the neighborhood, that wisdom is calling out in the streets, that God was at work before you got there, your task is listening—listening to join in with all the redemptive hopes of the people in your neighborhood. Imagine that every person who has meaningful hopes for some aspect of the new commons (social, economic, environmental, educational or civic well-being) is a potential partner in the reconciliation and renewal of the parish.

If you develop a sacred imagination for all of life and all of the people and systems living out the drama of their lives in the setting of your parish, then this everyday rooting process reveals astounding possibilities. But there is an adjustment that needs to be made, one that we are finding ultimately quite powerful. It requires even more humility; it's fair to say that when we change our imaginations to being in relationship with all that God is doing in a particular place, we become co-caretakers alongside our neighbors for the whole of the parish.

COLLABORATION BEATS COMPETITION

Rooting together within the parish is a gift in numerous ways. It helps to know that you are not alone when seeking its flourishing. But finding links within the parish also relieves anxieties and the undercurrent of competitiveness. Resources that seemed scarce may now seem abundant.

When you are scared—and scared for good reasons—it's easy to compare, defend and compete with other churches and ministries. You can begin to think this is how the game is played, that only the biggest and best survive. Just because this is not a posture Scripture calls us to doesn't mean it's not an easy mindset to slip into. But once you start comparing, you enter the vortex of scarcity. Before long, the posture and mindset of competition can take over and then it is nearly impossible to collaborate well. Ministry competition is an idol, and like all good idols it's tempting, it's destructive and it has an entire ecosystem propping it up.

For example, an all too common question among church leaders is, "How many are you running?" That is, "How many people come to your weekly gathering?" It's often the first question asked, and it's inherently a comparison question. Instantly in this relationship there is a winner and loser. There is a top and a bottom. What a tragedy when we so desperately need the encouragement, partnership and perspectives of one another! Now compare the competitive question of numbers to a more collaborative one. This is the beginning of a very different conversation:

- What do you see God doing in your neighborhood?
- What efforts are already underway to engage injustice?

- What gifts have you seen being leveraged in the community for the common good?

- What do you love about the neighborhood that you want to see grow?

See the difference? And, more importantly, do you feel the difference? When our outlook changes from scarcity to abundance it also changes the relational environment from one of competition to one of collaboration.

Everyone acknowledges that collaboration is a good idea in theory, but knowing what should happen and actually doing it are two different animals. If you are honest, it's a tragic reality that the majority of today's structures generate more competition than collaboration. Organizing around faithful presence in the parish disrupts this structure in a powerful way. The parish is simultaneously the scalpel knife to the infection of overgrown competition and the healing bandage of collaboration.

ROOTING WITH CREATION

Rooting together with all the people in your neighborhood is difficult enough to imagine. But what about partnering with the land and animals? What about collaborating with the creational and built environments? Does that give you the heebie-jeebies? Does it sound like hippy talk? Remember there is a reciprocal relationship here—we shape our places and then our places shape us.

When the young chief of the Cayuses tribe was signing over their lands to the US government in 1855, he said, "I wonder if the Ground has anything to say? I wonder if the ground is listening to what is said?"[5] As it turns out, the ground does listen, and eventually it does talk back. Charlene Spretnak's eye-opening book *The Resurgence of the Real* shows how "modern life promised freedom from the vagaries of the body, the limits of nature, and the provincial ties to place. The body came to be seen as a biological machine, the natural world as a mere externality in modern economies, and the sense of place as a primitive precursor to cosmopolitan sophistication." Now, just a couple centuries later, "the actual presence and power of body, nature, and place *are* now reasserting themselves and poking large holes through the modern ideologies of denial."[6]

Recovering a faithful reciprocal relationship with the created world is more encompassing than a typical understanding of creational stewardship. Most stewardship conversations stress the care of the earth and living systems. There is no doubt this is of vital importance. But a parish perspective helps us to see with fresh eyes. As a result we ask new questions. Ask yourself, *What might God be saying to us through this neighborhood? What do the buildings and zoning legislation reveal? What are the streams, air, forests, fields, parks, and even the resident animals, birds, insects and fish saying?* Your place matters. You are already in a dependent relationship with it. Yet the Western tendency is to live above our specific locations, as though the environment is meant to be our slave. Tragically, the good gift of God's creation is viewed and leveraged as nothing more than natural resources for human consumption.

We acknowledge that talking about strengthening your relational links to the creational and built environment may be new to some people. But there are practices throughout history with respect to this. Many indigenous communities measure and evaluate their use of the land based on how contemporary actions will affect the next seven generations. Do you have the vision to think that way about new housing construction, storefronts and parks? What about the way local farmers use crop rotation to develop the kind of soil that takes slow and careful preservation to remain fertile? Do you have the long-term vision to see the deep reciprocal relationship of your place? As you deepen your roots you will find yourself falling in love with your place. As your love grows so will your grief as you see land objectified or buildings neglected. You will question the wisdom of designing streets and alleys for cars more than for people.

As your love grows, so will your roots; as your roots grow so will your love.

ROOTING WITH THE BUILT ENVIRONMENT

Think for a moment about the phrase "church buildings." What are the church buildings in your place? If you are like most people, your mind doesn't immediately jump to all the homes, businesses, public spaces, fields and forests that comprise your neighborhood. But once the followers of Christ in a neighborhood begin to envision themselves as the local church instead of a building—once they see the parish as the place where they live out their faith—every building becomes a potential "church building." They all become sacred spaces for worship, mission, formation and community. Each one is one marked by our concern for their ongoing renewal and redemptive repurposing.

CONCLUSION

If the body of Christ is going to experience a movement of unity, then it desperately needs a new imagination for how the church can be rooted in the neighborhood in such a way that includes the particularity of all of our differences and the universality of our common faith.

If you begin with faithful presence in a geographic area, then in some sense this diverse, multilayered church is already there. Now they just need to be introduced to one another. Is this naive and simplistic? We thought so too until we started visiting neighborhoods. The three of us stumbled into pockets of Christians coming together around common hopes in neighborhoods everywhere we went. This thing is possible. And besides, the risk is worth it. Do you really want it to remain as it has always been?

As our friend Brandon Rhodes quips, "The body of Christ has become so dismembered that we don't have a leg to stand on."[7] This needs to change. The parish could be the literal ground that helps us to re-member. Set your grand visions of changing your neighborhood to the side, and instead focus your attention on listening to your place. Let your feet come to know and love your streets.

PRAYER FOR THE NEW PARISH

God of Faithful Presence,

Help us become people who love the particularity for how you created us. Free us to embrace our located particularity with the same kind of joy with which you give our particularity. Help us to love our place with your heart.

Amen.

CONVERSATIONS FOR THE NEW PARISH

- Are you a character in your neighborhood? A character is a person who is known, quirks and all. Share examples of characters you've known in your place. Wonder together about ways of rooting within your parish so people might come to know of and depend on you.

- Have a conversation with your community of faith exploring intentional ways of being present as a group in the life of your neighborhood.

- Share with a friend or two the realms of life you are most passionate about. Discuss what it might be like to join a group that already exists in your parish that shares this passion. How might you grow if you intentionally entered into the diversity of your place?

POSTURES AND PRACTICES FOR THE NEW PARISH

- **Localizing the things you already do:** What patterns of life might take on new significance when oriented back to the neighborhood? For example, joining local sports leagues, shopping, hanging out in cafés and pubs. It's important to remember that you don't need to add more activities to your life to be meaningfully rooted in place; simply increase your intention around where you do your activities so as to increase the opportunity to bump into neighbors and deepen local relationships.

- **Set programs aside for a season:** Christian groups sometimes create programs or new ministries in their effort to engage in collective action. Have a conversation with your community of faith about intentional ways of being present as a group in the life of your neighborhood without creating something new. Where and how do you play, hang out, serve? What is already present in your neighborhood that you might engage in with another person from your faith community?

- **Listen to love:** As you practice rooting in your place, set aside grand ideas to change or fix your place; instead focus on listening to your place so as to love it as Christ does. Imagine what your rooted presence might look like as your love for your neighborhood deepens.

8

Linking

Connecting the Church Across Places

Alone we can do so little;
together we can do so much.

Helen Keller

Most people rarely pause to consider how seemingly incon-
sequential patterns and structures of life shape them. But once
you realize it, you can slow down and reconsider what types of
habits and contexts might help you become more receptive to
the reality of God and the love of others. Both rooting deeply
in a place and linking wisely across places can be ways of
opening you to the truth and bringing about healing collaborations with others.

Although it can sound almost paradoxical, or at least counter-
intuitive, linking beyond your parish is vital for deep rooting.
And the rooting aspect is vital for meaningful linking. To illus-

trate the paradox, here are three fictional snapshots that reveal the dangers of living without either the rooting or the linking practice. They capture the three most common ways that Western cultural constructions distort our vision. We think of these distortions as forms of *spatial blindness*.

SNAPSHOT ONE: NEARSIGHTEDNESS

To the occasional outsider, the old fishing village had an idyllic sense about it: colorful verandas, waving palm trees and the romance of peeling paint on old, wooden fishing boats. But for Bonita, a dark-skinned mother of three in her forties who had lived her whole life inside the same routines and identities as the other townspeople, her place was filled with pain and emptiness.

Though she was a wise and innovative woman, she was obligated to carry out the same wearisome tasks that her mother had done, and her mother's mother before her. Carving, threading, shearing, weaving, tying and twisting, she wore her hands to the bone repairing fishing nets from daylight to dusk. But her rigorous days were a quiet reprieve from the suffering she faced in the late evenings.

Often her husband would return home from a bad day on the boats in a drunken rage. A single move in the wrong direction or a wrong glance of concern could set off a series of blows that would cause someone twice her size to double over. Her days were not pleasant by any means. But then again, it was not as though she regretted her situation. This was how it had always been; this was the lot in life for a woman of her position.

• • •

Throughout human history Bonita's form of nearsightedness has been the most common by far. When a person is nearsighted they can only see what is close at hand, needing a corrective lens to see what lies further out. In a similar way, people suffering from nearsightedness with respect to place are cocooned in their little corner of the world. Those suffering this way have lived their lives in an enclosed place and are stuck with their biases and cultural blind spots. Traditionally this arises from societies with deep tribal identities or kinship circles based on bloodlines. It also happens in rural contexts that are separated from the flow of newcomers and travelers that are so common in more urban contexts. In the modern world this blindness is forced upon vast populations who suffer needlessly under abject poverty and immobility.

SNAPSHOT TWO: FARSIGHTEDNESS

As a professor of sociology at the University of Berkeley (along with holding a number of prestigious chairs around the globe), Archer Hoffman had been privileged to travel the world identifying people groups and studying their social relations. There was one thing Archer was sure he had discovered over the course of his life. In order to have a liberal and generous outlook, an open mind, and a tolerant capacity toward others, you had to go places. You had to see the world, explore diverse cultures and meet people who saw the world differently.

While he had a kind of smugness toward the more insular types back home—with their fundamentalist convictions and lack of tolerance—Archer had to admit he occasionally felt a deep sense of loneliness. There was a sweeping feeling that some hidden realm of relational wisdom and deep groundedness was missing from his life. He felt a sense of growing unease regarding his cosmopolitan ways.

In his later travels, Archer found himself watching the way

various tribes attuned themselves to the land and to each other; the way certain villagers functioned with such a natural sense of interdependent care. It was as if the time and years of community life and deep connection to place had brought with it a unity and sensibility that could never be fully digested by the outside observer.

• • •

Archer Hoffman suffered from farsightedness. People suffering from farsightedness can clearly see things from a distance but are blind to what is right in front of them. This form of spatial blindness began to pick up steam during the industrial revolution as the cost of travel went down, and opportunities for new experiences went up. The ease of travel makes it possible for those with even moderate wealth to explore other cultures while living under the illusion that they have seen the world from a neutral scientific perspective above the fray of cultural bias.

Archer was "open-minded" and understood the world from multiple perspectives. But he was never rooted in one place long enough to learn the deeply relational wisdom that comes from caring for a common geography together over the course of time. Therefore Archer lived above place in a way that perpetuated his loneliness, blindness and fragmentation.

SNAPSHOT THREE: DOUBLE VISION

Samia Mohandas set her iTunes playlist for the twenty-two minute commute to work at the Seattle-Tacoma Airport. She didn't mind the drive. In some ways she felt like she was living the dream. At twenty-six years old she was already working as a flight attendant for Horizon Air. She had two condos, one in Seattle and one in Denver (her primary flight stop). Well, she didn't exactly own them, she rented. And the condo in Seattle was actually in Federal Way, an outlying suburban hub in close proximity to her work.

There were times, though, when her drive down 320th toward the freeway onramp made her feel paradoxically both "at home" and in "the middle of nowhere"—it had the same stores, same arterials, same restaurants, same hotels and the same condos she had seen replicated in nearly every city she had visited around the country. In fact, once while daydreaming she had driven by the Federal Way strip mall and made a wrong turn thinking she was actually in Denver.

No matter. Once she made it to the I-5 highway she could occupy her time with more important things than strip-mall homogeny. You didn't really have to pay attention to the place at all once you were in the flow of traffic. You just had to ensure you didn't collide with the car in front of you. The highway was critical space for her daily online routine.

Samia was proud of her multitasking abilities—the capacity to stay plugged in, linked up and synced together. She could pound a couple dozen text messages, answer a few emails and check her social networks (for her it was Facebook, Twitter, LinkedIn, Pinterest and Instagram) all within the scope of her twenty-two-minute commute. Sometimes, though, it all felt a little surreal, like everything had a shiny veneer. Like her aunt liked to say about modern life, "there is no *there* there". . . or like that electronic billboard for the cell phone company that she passed by on the last off-ramp before the airport that read, "BE CONNECTED EVERYWHERE, EVEN IN THE MIDDLE OF NOWHERE!"

· · ·

Double vision is a relatively new form of spatial blindness that has become a viral epidemic only in the last fifty years. The problem starts when a society develops the habit of using their context (or tools in that context) as a medium to be somewhere else. Organizing life this way for generations leads to structures that keep you separated and distracted from developing lasting or meaningful connections with your local place or people.

Samia's story illustrates this in many ways. Everything has been constructed to capitalize on her attention. All the things she might have found within the context of community she must now find elsewhere. For example, take a look at the car-dominated streetscape, the media-saturated bubble and the built constructs that dictate her capacity to be present. Over the course of time, forces like these converged in a way that disconnected Samia's hold on what was real.

In her case the "neighborhoods" where her condos were located didn't allow more than one type of use. This means residential plots could be built, but all other life activities, like shopping, working, eating out, going to the library and even going to school, were beyond walking distance. In many places, communities where a person can live, work and play within walkable distances are becoming essentially illegal due to zoning regulations or impossible due to their structure.

Samia also has a myriad of tools and technologies competing for her attention, impairing her ability to be fully present. "The very structure of media fosters fragmentation and furnishes isolated images. Without continuity and context, we can't integrate information bits into any sort of whole."[1] It is this swirl of speeding digital distractions that causes Samia to feel, as the great "prophet of speed" Paul Virilio describes it, "everywhere and nowhere, here and elsewhere, neither inside or outside. . . .

[An] obligatory tele-presence is submerging the immediate presence of individuals . . . [and] supplanting the vision of the real world around us."[2]

When all these structures and technologies begin converging, we end up living in a world that is constructed to keep our attention away from the kind of connections necessary for real community relations to develop. Being present in the place we live becomes impossible. But we rarely notice it because, as the Quaker theorist Ursula Franklin has said, it becomes "just the way we do things around here."

As this way of life becomes a global epidemic, it also becomes more and more difficult to make meaningful connections with other local cultures, parishes and people. The homogeneity of global culture dominates, and most everything has a certain sameness about it. Local differences that remain are co-opted and become spectacle, tourism, entertainment and consumption options. In this type of environment we have to get very intentional about both our local practice of rooting in the parish and our wider practice of linking with real places.

LINKING AS AN INDIVIDUAL, AS A CHURCH AND AS A PARISH

Linking connections are important to make individually, as a faith community and even collectively as a parish. Every community should hope to live into a practice of both rooting and linking. Even someone called to deep local practice should maintain some bonds across places. In the same way, those who are called to emphasize the linking and networking aspects should maintain a local practice as a character in the neighborhood.

When faith communities develop transparent and collaborative links across places, they become healthier as a team. This health grows their capacity to bring healing to others. Once the church you are a part of begins to embrace its collective responsibilities and limitations within the parish an inevitable question arises: "What are our responsibilities outside of our own parish, and how will linking across places form us in connection with the larger body of Christ?" This is illustrated throughout the epistles as Paul connects the joys and struggles of the church in one parish to that of another, calling for mutual responsibility and prayerful support.

The people in your neighborhood may be interested in joining in on some of these linking practices too. Imagine your town, village or parish developing sister relationships with other neighborhoods around the world. Or perhaps there are adjacent parishes you could be collaborating with on related problems or possibilities.

LINKING ACROSS GEOGRAPHIES

Acts 1:8 says, "But you will receive power when the Holy Spirit comes on you; and you will be my witnesses in Jerusalem, and in all Judea and Samaria, and to the ends of the earth." Luke offers a helpful guide for framing the geographical possibilities associated with linking beyond your own parish.

First, Jerusalem—linking across city. There is an important mutual responsibility to embrace those parishes that are in immediate proximity to your own. In this global age, it doesn't take a genius to recognize that your local actions can have city-wide, regional and even global effects. But typically those parishes closest to you are the ones affected most deeply by your community's choices. Partnering across neighborhoods in the city or county exposes areas of insularity and opens the door for reconciliation, collaboration and innovation.

Second, Judea and Samaria—linking across the region. There are important linkages to be made at the regional level as well. Some might refer to this as *bioregional linking*. Those in the same climate and cultural region often have similar problems and possibilities that make sharing best practices especially useful for each other. This approach is a much more fruitful means of learning than centralized planning where experts offer top-down procedures that transcend the contextual dynamics of time and place. This is often true whether it comes from the powers of state or the expertise of multinational corporations. But this concern is especially relevant for religious denominations and networks that institute directives across boundaries without contextual care.

Finally, the ends of the earth—linking across the globe. There are critical global links to be made. These can be the most profound and the most difficult. Usually they are the links that highlight cultural differences the most, and the added dimension of distance makes them difficult to hold onto. A parish that develops reciprocal relationships across the globe may soon find itself forming views about the world that diverge immensely from others in its area. There is nothing like getting out of your comfort zone and developing reciprocal friendships across borders to awaken people to unique cultural realities.

It's for this exact reason the Parish Collective has formed a partnership with the Global Immersion Project. While the directors, Jon Huckins and Jer Swigart, have deep commitment in their own parishes, they understand the tremendous value of crosscultural immersion. Each year teams travel to Israel and Palestine to learn from peacemaking leaders in particular neighborhoods living right in the middle of the tensions between this ancient conflict. When participants return, they find that their leadership in their own communities is transformed by what they experienced across the world.

LINKING WITH AFFINITIES

In the introduction we mentioned that Paul's church went from hundreds to a handful when they moved from a consumer church toward one that rooted itself in and for a particular neighborhood. It wasn't long before this little group in Tacoma began to realize how much they needed encouragement. to feel that they weren't alone. Paul started driving members of the church to tour other parishes or attend meetings led by other practitioners. He would highlight stories from books of people who were living the parish way in other countries. The church brought in guests from other cities and neighborhoods for inspiration and support. Since that time they have started eight social enterprises and small businesses in the neighborhood, collaborated with others on a multitude of projects that have brought grassroots renewal, and offered inspiration to others groups struggling to survive.

It's vital to link beyond your own parish with those who share an affinity. The consequence of these linking connections stimulate encouragement, belonging, hope and innovation. Linking across places restores your hope and encourages you that it is possible to live with deeper roots in your place. So pay attention. There are stories of struggle and of God's intervention in other places that could mean the world to you. Your connections with others practicing parish with similar desires can help your faith stay alive. This can never be underestimated.

LINKING WITH DIVERSITIES

The first year of the Inhabit Conference, participants were introduced to plenary speakers Majora Carter and Brenda Salter McNeil. Both of these African American women are incredible leaders, and their presentations had all of us begging for more.

While their areas of expertise around themes of neighborhood and community are quite diverse, there was one issue they both emphasized as crucial. Women should travel more—and not just travel, but experience the life and culture of other places. You have to understand, the Inhabit Conference brings local heroes from around North America to talk about their commitment to staying. But both of these women, who are renowned for localism and reconciliation, were telling women to get out more. It was a little surprising to everyone.

As Majora and Brenda began to explain themselves, their reasoning became quite clear. Many women around the world have excelled in their commitment to building relationships, caring for others and growing the relational fabric within their particular context. Often (and perhaps especially so for African American women) they have not had the freedom and mobility to travel and experience the world from other perspectives. Over the course of generations, many women (and men) that are born into insular environments of patriarchy or racism may assume that this is just the way things are, or even the way they are meant to be.

Majora and Brenda were calling on these women to risk getting out and experiencing the tremendous possibility that comes from developing connections to other cultures and ways of doing things. Only by linking with other places would they be able to see all the unique ways of overcoming oppression. Immersed in new stories, they might discover how valuable their relational efforts really are, what kind of leadership they are capable of, and that another way of living might be possible.

Forming bonds across diverse places can expand your capacity for solidarity and collaboration. Intentionally developing relationships with communities that are culturally different than your own parish forms you as a person who can delight in the rich diversity of God's creation. The cultural biases and blind spots that all humans naturally develop over the course of generations are confronted by experiencing other ways of doing things. Linking with others, especially those who are different can be understood as longing for the truth, specifically, the truth about how your ways of acting and relating are healing or hurting others.

LINKING ACROSS TIME AND SPACE

The final linking mode is linking across time and space. This is not the *Star Trek* section where you engage in futuristic time travel. It simply means developing practices that help you connect to both the church universal and the stories of diverse cultures across generations and across borders.

Linking across time and space means connecting as best you can with those generations that came before you, both within the church and without. Exploring old books, listening to the stories of your elders, and reflecting deeply on the Scriptures will enlarge your life, encourage your heart and keep you awake to the biases that develop during particular eras. C. S. Lewis once said, "It is a good rule, after reading a new book, never to allow yourself another new one till you have read an old one in between."[3] While the three of us heartily recommend completing the book you have in front of you now, the instruction remains relevant.

The more you immerse yourself in the stories of Scripture, the more you will find yourself living as though you are not alone. The apostle Paul writes, "Since we are surrounded by such a great cloud of witnesses, let us throw off everything that hinders and the sin that so easily entangles. And let us run with perseverance the race marked out for us" (Hebrews 12:1). It is important to develop the kind of imagination and faith that is capable of seeing yourself connected to the church's past, present and future across space and time. The Scriptures, when read with a listening ear, illuminate various forms of blindness, inspire perseverance and hold us as characters with a storied past and a life-giving future.

PRAYER FOR THE NEW PARISH

God of All Creation,

Give us vision to see our true need of one another. And give us the courage to link beyond the comfort of what we know and understand so that we might discover and come to love the diversity of your creation.

Amen.

CONVERSATIONS FOR THE NEW PARISH

- As you reflect on the three types of spatial blindness (nearsightedness, farsightedness and double vision), which of the three captures your personal quest to see your place?

- Explore potential dangers of becoming siloed within your own neighborhood. Why are both rooting and linking necessary for faithful presence? What might happen if you and your group only rooted or only linked?

- Describe the profile of your neighborhood. What kinds of groups or neighborhoods does your neighborhood most need to be in relationship with? What if your new parish church fostered a mutually beneficial relationship with a group in a neighborhood from a different economic class or racial/ethnic mix or urban/rural/suburban identity, etc.?

POSTURES AND PRACTICES FOR THE NEW PARISH

- **New parish learning journey:** Go on a pilgrimage to visit another faith community in a different parish, either across town or in another city. Walk their streets and get to know some people who live within that parish. How is their faith community seeking to be faithfully present within their place?

- **Commission unto place:** When people leave your faith community, help them identify rooted faith communities where they are going. Rather than just saying goodbye, mark their leaving as a sending to new adventures of faithful presence in a new place. This can be a powerful way of maintaining friendship while developing a meaningful link to another parish.

- **Sharing stories of faithful presence:** Invite people from other parishes to an evening of storytelling. Don't just invite the big stories of neighborhood renewal, but encourage the sharing of the little things normal people are doing. By sharing what God is doing through regular people in various neighborhoods your group will see how significant their seemingly mundane personal practices can be. This can be a powerful practice that both seeds each other's parish imaginations and creates opportunities to celebrate and bless one another.

9

Leading

Living a Life Worth Following

If you want to discover and discern what God is up to in the world just now, stop trying to answer the question from within the walls of your churches. Like strangers in need of hospitality who have left their baggage behind, enter the neighborhoods and communities where you live. Sit at the table of the other, and there you may begin to hear what God is doing.

Alan J. Roxburgh, *Missional: Joining God in the Neighborhood*

We can't solve problems by using the same kind of thinking we used when we created them.

Albert Einstein

The vast array of modern definitions and understandings of leadership are so woven into the psyches of the Western world that our first step toward learning to lead others in this parish transition is to begin with a new question altogether. Instead of asking, "What would a leader do in this context?" or "What are the qualities of a leader I need to adopt?" we must begin by asking, "What is worth following?" While this simple question is often overlooked in leadership resources, it will form our exploration of leadership in the new parish.

Asking, "What is worth following?" is a helpful antidote to our cultural inclination to look for certain caricatures of a leader that may have very little to do with healing relationships, stewarding the land or anything else related to God's redemptive vision. If we allow the broader culture to predetermine the qualities of a leader, we can easily overlook the very gifts, skills and character qualities that God desires for us to discover. These caricatures of leaders are what caused the Pharisees of Jesus' day to miss the appearance of the Messiah. Think about that for a moment.

Sometimes the Pharisees get sort of a bad rap because of how incredibly serious they were about following the Torah and how nit-picky they could be. But they desperately wanted to identify the Messiah, probably more than the average Israelite, and yet many of them missed Christ because of what they thought they should be looking for. Do we suffer from the same problem? Without realizing it, we can easily assume the wrong definitions and make false assumptions regarding what a leader is supposed to accomplish. Consider how the conversation shifts when we ask the following questions:

- Who are the people in my parish who have learned to bring together diverse parties in peace and reconciliation?

- Who are those people who consistently demonstrate the art of hospitality, generosity and compassion to the stranger?

- Where are the people in my group who have learned how to work through conflict, fitting together as a team that is greater than the sum of the parts?

- What neighbors weave a fabric of love and care throughout the parish through humble acts of kindness and appreciative conversations?

In each of the above questions the most important issue is the personal practice of faithful presence. Quite simply, there is no way to lead well if we have not developed a personal practice in the neighborhood. There is no faking it. A charismatic demeanor and polished speeches will only go so far. In the neighborhood, character is king.

Neighborhood and missional leader Daniel White Jr. has said, "We've convinced ourselves we can become experts without practical exposure."[1] In other words, it's too easy to elevate people as leaders who are not really skilled in the very basic practice of being human, let alone the task of leadership. Just because a person is extroverted, has lots of innovative ideas or is a compelling communicator does not necessarily mean he or she is worth following. This may not be the case everywhere, but in the parish, authority requires the fruits of the Spirit.

With Jesus, the gospel and the fruits of the Spirit in mind, keep asking: What's worth following? People who have learned to practice faithful presence are worth following. This is so important and yet so overlooked, particularly in the church. It's amazing how simply asking this question can awaken you to a whole spectrum of people who have often been marginalized or overlooked. A few examples include:

- the elderly

- people without homes

- the racially oppressed

- children

- formerly incarcerated women and men

The first and most critical dimension of leading groups in this transition is learning to listen to and follow those who have already learned to practice faithful presence in your context. This can be a humbling and difficult move for those in a "leadership" position. Yet, the best way to develop a personal practice is to listen and follow those who already have one. Consider finding someone who does not fit the traditional description of a leader but who demonstrates faithful presence. What could you learn from this person? How could you honor their actions by listening and incorporating their habits in your own life?

Developing a personal practice of becoming faithfully present in your neighborhood is vital. You cannot ask this of others if you are not moving in that direction yourself. While the process can be complex, and may demand great risk-taking faith, at the core it is still a simple premise. Ask yourself, *What personal practices can help me move toward common life, common mission and common formation together with the body of Christ in the neighborhood?* Examples may include:

- consistent participation in your local community council

- spending more time in leisure in your own neighborhood instead of going across town

- frequenting local coffee shops, businesses and restaurants, and getting to know the owners

- prayerfully walking your own neighborhood with eyes to how God is at work

- being a trusted older friend to kids in the neighborhood and encouraging their parents

This is not to say that there are not important qualities and characteristics beyond developing your personal practice of faithful presence. But it does mean there is a correlation between developing your practice in the neighborhood and faithfully fulfilling your leadership calling. With that in mind, we can more helpfully consider leadership as it relates to the new parish.

OLD DEFINITIONS OF LEADERSHIP HAVE TO GO

When the three of us are sharing about the new parish vision with groups around North America it doesn't take long for people to claim that for them to make this radical transition, it's going to require finding more leaders and better leadership. Often we will ask those who make this claim to offer some words that describe what they mean when they say the word *leadership*. Many will use words like *charismatic, motivator, communicator, knowledgeable, risk taker* and *inspirational*. Inevitably someone might quote some leadership guru saying something like "The true measure of leadership is influence—nothing more, nothing less." A leader is someone who can get others to carry out the vision, is it not?

But then we often ask some unsettling questions: Do you think Hitler was a leader? Was Hitler not one of the most influential leaders of the twentieth century? And if so, do you still think we need more leaders? When we ask these questions, the tension in the room is palpable. Sometimes there are even gasps of horror, as if we had set a trap for them that was now causing considerable pain. Some argue that Hitler was a leader, but backpedal regarding the need for more like him. Others argue that Hitler was not a leader, but cannot reconcile the fact that he was able to wield tremendous influence and had millions of followers.

There is tension here because of the way most people have come to conceive of leadership. On the one hand, it requires a certain way of treating others. And on the other hand, we see it as a set of abstract qualities without any values attached. As Ronald Heifetz from the Leadership School at Harvard reminds us:

> We cannot continue to have it both ways. We may like to use the word *leadership* as if it were value-free, particularly in an age of science and mathematics. . . . Yet when we do so, we ignore the other half of ourselves that in the next breath speaks of leadership as something we desperately need more of. We cannot talk about a crisis in leadership and then say leadership is value-free.[2]

This is an important note. It's simply not fair to equate leadership with influence. In fact, allowing leadership to be synonymous with influence in such a celebrity-driven and self-obsessed culture as ours is downright dangerous. With this in mind, we define leadership as *the capacity to mobilize desire for reconciliation and renewal through collective action, while paying ongoing attention to God's story, to the fidelity of the group within its place and to the leader's own transformation.* As this definition reflects, there is a now-and-not-yet dialectic in leadership. Leaders develop the capacity to draw others toward faithful presence together as they discern their way into a faithful future. True leaders can never compromise their own faithful presence in the hope of drawing others together, or in the hope of achieving their future end.

METAPHORS MATTER

As you shift your attention to the question "What is worth following?" not only do new leaders become visible, but you find new metaphors for leadership emerging as well. The metaphors that are used for leadership make a big difference. Hundreds of thousands of people in neighborhoods are leading in powerful ways that contribute to the shalom of God, but they don't count themselves as leaders because of the metaphors they've adopted. Likewise, it's quite possible for positional "leaders" in various fields to mistakenly believe they should be seen as leaders in the neighborhood based on their status and outside expertise.

This dynamic might sound familiar by now. One group shirks responsibility, the other transcends limitations, and for both it is a consequence of how they view leadership. With this in mind, here are three metaphors for reimagining leadership in the new parish. By no means are these metaphors exhaustive. But, from our experience, if you are seeking to nurture and mobilize neighborhood renewal, each of these metaphors will help you practice a new way of leading. They also allow a progression that the three of us have seen all those who are leading well in the new parish adopt in some form. Our intent here is not to define areas of gifting, but to offer word pictures that spark our imagination toward a new vision of leadership.

The Designer: Shaping environments and practices to bring people together. The *designer* configures experiments and reshapes environments that make it easy for neighbors to come together. These are contexts where it's easy for people to get to know one another. These are tweaks in current structures that help outsiders feel like insiders or desecrated spaces to become sacred again. Functioning as a designer allows the leader to look at the whole parish and ask, "What could we reshape that would help bring people together and alter their imagination of what's possible?"

With the modern emphasis on rationality, most have grossly underestimated the power of the designing formative environments that facilitate transformation and healing. As Richard Rohr often says, "We do not think ourselves into a new kind of living. We live ourselves into a new kind of thinking." Sometimes these adaptations can be quite small, like redesigning the living room to be more open and inviting for neighborhood visitors of all income levels. Or it might be something much larger, such as turning a vacant piece of property into a public gathering space.

One of the heroes of neighborhood renewal is artist and place-making guru Candy Chang. A few years ago Candy's mother became ill and eventually died from cancer. Throughout the process the theme of death kept pressing toward the front of Candy's thoughts. *What types of things does a person wish to do before they die?* Knowing time was short, Candy also started to think through how she wanted to spend her last days with her mom.

In Candy's neighborhood in New Orleans there was one particular house that had been boarded up and left as an abandoned and unusable space. After a period of dreaming about what could be done to honor her mother and reconfigure public space, Candy came up with a brilliant plan. She used a special type of paint that turned a side of the house into a giant chalkboard. Then she drew out the words "Before I die, I want to _____." Over and over she wrote these words across the entire wall. She left a box of chalk for those who might pass by. Then she waited. Before long people of all ages, sizes and backgrounds were filling in the blank spaces with their longings. Soon the wall was full of wonderful dreams and hopes. Today there are walls turned to chalkboards with word experiments inspired by Candy all over the world.

In one meaningful act of architectural imagination Candy reshaped both the environment and the way people used the space. The designer understands that the medium matters. The context is formative. The environment is a big deal when it comes to faithful presence. Candy used her design skill to reshape a seemingly ordinary space. In turn, this shifted her neighbors' experience. This is leadership. Candy embraced the pain of her mother's death in a way that not only was true to her as a person but mobilized others to give voice to some of their deepest hopes for life, while simultaneously transforming a neighborhood eyesore into a gathering place of inspiration.

It's not surprising to us that that so many of our most inspiring models of leading as designers are women. Historically men have often glamorized the structures that emphasize separation, individuality, power, indestructibility and wealth. Women, however, have excelled for centuries at creating and designing environments for deeper shared life, performing cosmetic repairs to the shape of homes, storefronts and community centers so they might be more hospitable for flourishing together.

Often our best guides have been bravely leading, but because their contributions don't fit our definitions, they're too often missed or neglected. In all our intellectual smarts, we miss the deep wisdom that lies waiting to be discovered. How do we find it? Patricia Talton (Paul's previous boss at the Northwest Leadership Foundation) told the crowd at TEDx Tacoma: "Well I say we reach back. We reach back through the ages and grab a hold of wisdom. I think she's waiting. Proverbs says that wisdom calls out to the streets. She raises her voice in the public square. Let's reach for her. Let's invite her."[3]

Today many forms of modern city planning are awakening to the ways women have led the way in designing structures for human engagement and care of the created world. It's another example of why we need to pay close attention to our blind spots when asking the question "What's worth following?"

To sum up, the designer catalyzes shared life in the neighborhood by:

- *Reshaping environments.* As you walk your neighborhood with your friends, what ideas are sparked that could be a new initiative or practice? What buildings, associations or other aspects of your neighborhood are in need of a design makeover?

- *Curating strategic connections.* How might you help mobilize your friends and neighbors around renewal opportunities?

- *Configuring experiments.* How might you help others support, resource, encourage and celebrate the designer—to move beyond the realm of "It would it be cool if . . ." to taking action to design greater beauty into your place?

If the designer is one who shapes environments and convenes new practices, then the conductor invites the unique voices in this environment or experiment toward meaningful contribution. The conductor continually teases out the strengths of each member and creatively encourages them toward authenticity and harmonization.

The Conductor: Orchestrating the parts to function as a whole. The *conductor* is a metaphor that draws out some of the most critical skills for helping integrate co-creators and co-stewards more faithfully in the parish. The conductor helps each person discover her or his unique role and how that calling contributes to the overall symphonic resonance of the group. In a band or orchestra, the conductor draws out the gifts and strengths of each musician so that each is working at the edge of their skill but not beyond their capability. Each instrument has a voice in the arrangement, and none should overwhelm and drown out another, except when the music invites a solo.

The conductor is not looking to offer the one-size-fits-all answer from the command and control center. Instead, she seeks to facilitate the flow, to awaken presence, to help all parties enter in fully aware of their unique limits and responsibilities. She is a savvy facilitator and understands leadership as a form of faithful engagement that helps move players toward fitting together as a team moving toward beauty and goodness. The person in this role understands leadership as an active way of being, not a static position of authority. In fact, the conductor encourages leadership from all parties, calling them to be fully present to their role in drawing the group toward synergistic harmony. Sharon Daloz Parks is worth quoting at length here:

> When the focus shifts from authority and technical problems to leadership and making progress on adaptive challenges, the charisma and the traits of the individual personality may become less critical. In this view, acts of leadership depend less on the magnetism and social dominance of heroic individuals and more on the capacities of individuals (who may be located in a wide variety of positions) to skillfully intervene in complex systems. The multifaceted capacity to be present becomes a key factor in effective leadership: the quality of one's capacity to be fully present, comprehend what is happening, hold steady in the field of action, and make choices regarding when and how to intervene from within the social group (from wherever you sit) in ways that help the group make progress on swamp issues.[4]

Wendy McCaig is an embodiment of the conductor metaphor in her work with the Hillside neighborhood in Richmond, Virginia.

As she walked through Hillside years ago, her heart was broken by the unsettling institutionalization of the place with little regard for the human soul. Most of the area consisted of a dismal low-income housing complex that had instituted codes of conduct, making things worse instead of better. Just a few of the variables rendering Hillside a bleak place included:

- It was surrounded by abandoned warehouses and industrial parks.

- Public spaces had been closed down.

- The unemployment rate was close to eighty percent.

- Trash was strewn all over the streets, and buildings needed maintenance.

- One small playground, serving over six hundred children, was in desperate need of repair.

- No community gardens or garden plots of any kind were allowed.

- There were no grocery store or mixed-use areas within walkable distance.

- Buses required two transfers to get to basic services.

- Fifty percent of the male population had been in prison at least once.

- Many men were living in the neighborhood "off book" and were resistant to getting involved.

Wendy began by reopening the neighborhood recreation center and being present in the daily life of the neighborhood herself. Soon she began to meet people and discover their unique gifts, talents, resources and passions. She listened for how the

Spirit was already at work and joined in support and encouragement. But then in the first three weeks of January 2011, there were three shootings resulting in three deaths. Weeks later, two teenagers were struck by stray bullets and injured. These were devastating tragedies.

After the shootings, Wendy went to those she had been growing relationships with and asked, "Who is ready to take back this neighborhood?" Patrice was ready. Patrice was well respected, street smart, passionate and incredibly bold. Wendy recognized her potential as a leader. Patrice started a support group for parents who wanted to keep children safe. Then things really got moving. Denise, who had a gift for hospitality, began preparing monthly meals, which served as a way of engaging the entire neighborhood. Lindsey expressed a desire to work with the girls in the neighborhood through cheerleading. John volunteered to help start a computer lab. Johnny helped start container gardens. Mrs. Murphy knew that the senior adults were a stabilizing force in this community and began a senior support group. They all worked together to start a mobile food pantry and organize job mentoring.

Tony saw what the others were doing and expressed his desire to form a football team, so they all worked together to make it happen. Through the football effort, Tony did what no one else was able to do. He got the men involved. Then something amazing happened: the football team drew the neighborhood together. It was one thing Hillside could really be proud of. Along the way, Wendy found local churches and nonprofits who cared about the same issues as her Hillside friends, and she started several missional communities to support the wonderful work being done. Together this team of neighborhood leaders and partners is a great example of collaboration.

Wendy exemplifies the role of the orchestra conductor. She

brought people together to work in harmony on Hillside's problems and possibilities, drawing out the unique contribution of each and every person and forming a band of players who fit together in ways that brought flourishing to the whole. This is what the conductor does, leaning into opportunities for renewal through the unique voice and gifting of each member of the parish in order that they may function together on behalf of the whole. The challenges for a conductor are to:

- *Discern your place's melody.* What is the song your neighborhood is trying to sing? As you walk through your area, look for the gifts your neighbors already express, and prayerfully invite those gifts to be shared for the benefit of the whole neighborhood; the melody is already there, and you can help them hear it.

- *Keep the beat.* How can you help your group live on or near the edge of faithful presence without drifting into the two temptations of transcending limitations (doing what's beyond them) or avoiding true responsibility (not doing what is uniquely theirs to do)?

- *Help members reimagine how their gifts contribute to the whole.* Consider the characters who have already demonstrated even small acts of blessing the neighborhood. How can you meaningfully honor their faithfulness while encouraging them to keep going? Never underestimate the power of noticing another person's efforts and blessing them.

If the designer is a shaper of environments and the conductor draws multiple voices into harmonious action, then the next metaphor for leadership within the new parish is the player/coach.

Player/Coach: Encouraging team members without leaving the game. In the parish there is no such thing as a leader who is not also a practitioner. The implication of being a member in the neighborhood is that you are responsible to act like one. To be a part of the living body of Christ does not diminish this task; rather, it magnifies it. The modern notion of a leader being someone who knows how to manage or inspire others with the right words while they carry out the necessary tasks to achieve the objectives is a gross reduction of Christian leadership. This is similar to the modern scientist who might think of herself as detached from the subject, capable of objective examination without changing the nature of the subject or the environment.

The *player/coach* is a critical leadership metaphor because it signifies that any coaching offered comes from someone who not only has played many games before but is in the game right now. Jesus' interactions with the religious leaders of his day underscore the importance of being wary of those who claim mastery of theory but can only offer instructions from the sidelines. In addition, the player/coach has a unique sensitivity and skill for tapping into both the head and the heart of the matter. In the midst of a difficult game, there is a delicate balance between combining emotional support with compelling incentive to give it one's all.

The three of us have turned time and again to the guidance of our dear mentor Michael Frost (one of the elders of the contemporary missional church movement) for the simple fact that Michael is not just a charismatic speaker and a brilliant author and storyteller; he is a lifetime resident and community leader in his parish of Manly in Sydney, Australia. He has been following Jesus into his neighborhood for more than fifty years. His missional teaching is grounded in a lifetime of rooted practice in Manly. In his most recent book *Incarnate: The Body of Christ in an Age of Disengagement*, Michael writes:

> I believe Christians should be the most rooted people in their community; their loyalty and devotion to a particular

geographical area and everyone who lives there should be legendary. I live in the neighborhood where I grew up. I have deep, long-term connections with the place and with the community. . . . And I drastically limit the amount of travel I do to ensure that my primary energy goes into the local.[5]

Michael has been a player/coach for us. Over the past decade there have been multiple occasions, whether hanging out with a few friends at a celebration or addressing larger groups from a stage, when we have been coached to stay in the game by Michael. And we stayed in the game in part because we knew he was still in the game. His consistent personal practice lends credibility to his words.

Michael has learned to engage both the head and the heart at the right strategic moment. A leader can shape environments and bring people together to collaborate all day long, but in the end the leader must have the courage and the wisdom to encourage people to keep going. A player/coach can listen to the heart of those in their group, discern what the group needs to persevere and act on what they discern. Sometimes a person or a group simply needs to be reminded of what an honor it is to follow Jesus, or that his or her contributions to the group truly are vital.

The player/coach has learned that there are "player" skills, emotions, resonances and so on, that come from being in the middle of the game, and there are "coaching" skills that come from stepping back, standing above the fray and evaluating what's going on from a larger perspective. And, most importantly, when the tactics of an active player are conjoined with the wisdom and perspective of a coach, a group has a leader—though never perfect—who can be trusted.

The player/coach demonstrates personal investment coupled with wisdom and perspective to compel a church or a neighborhood group to stay the course. As a rundown of the player/ coach, this leader of the new parish:

- *Is always a practitioner.* Prayerfully reflect on how and why you followed Christ into the realm of leadership that you are in. What are the vital practices that you know, deep in your heart, make you the kind of person truly worth following? How might you risk putting even more skin in the game?

- *Inspires both the head and the heart.* As you listen to the current health of your church or group, in your heart and mind what do you discern they most need? What is the trajectory of their energy level? What do they most need to stay the course of faithful presence?

- *Can play the game while also holding a larger field of vision.* Given that wisdom is born of rooting and linking over time, how can you gift your experience as a leader to those in your group? This kind of coaching is most powerful when you come alongside a person or a group of people at the right moment and speak into their deepest need. No technique can guide you into this. Fortunately we have something better: the Holy Spirit.

The new parish calls forth a new way of leading. It doesn't change the need for leadership. Leadership is always going to be necessary. The task of pastoring a group of people into this new vision may very well be the leadership challenge of the twenty-first-century church.

PRAYER FOR THE NEW PARISH

God of All,

Guide us into your way of leading. Teach us to fully enter our place as you entered the world in Christ Jesus.

Thank you for showing us a life worth following and give us the eyes to see those in our neighborhood whose worthy lives and actions we may have missed.

Amen.

CONVERSATIONS FOR THE NEW PARISH

- What makes a life worth following?

- In this chapter we define Christian leadership within the new parish as "the capacity to mobilize desire for reconciliation and renewal through collective action, while paying ongoing attention to God's story, to the fidelity of the group within its place and to the leader's own transformation." What does this understanding of leadership stir within you? Who might qualify as a leader? How is this similar to or different than the way your community of faith currently conceives of leadership?

- As you hold your parish in your heart, what combination of leadership metaphors (designer, conductor and player/coach) is most needed within your church for your group to become even more faithfully present within your neighborhood?

POSTURES AND PRACTICES FOR THE NEW PARISH

- **Lead out of personal practice:** As basic as this sounds, never forget the power of living a life worth following. The practices you engage—whether intentionally or precritically—shape who you become. As you seek to love God by loving your neighbor you will become a person worth following.

- **Notice and celebrate lives worth following:** Develop a practice of noticing and celebrating new parish leadership by people within your church and neighborhood who take risks unto faithful presence with others. Honor the people who have been faithful over the long haul in your neighborhood. Celebrate those who are stepping into their place with increased intention. Bless those who are bringing others together unto mutual flourishing.

- **God is already in your place:** Remember that God is and has been at work in your neighborhood. Part of leading is attuning yourself to the breath of God bringing new life to the dry bones of your place. Live in the freedom that comes from knowing that God loves your neighborhood far more than you ever will. You actually can trust God's love for your place.

Conclusion

Presence in a Post-Everything Future

*Peace be with you! As the Father has
sent me, I am sending you.*

Jesus, in John 20:21

Like us, you live in a world simultaneously growing more local
and more global. As we rocket toward this peculiar future together the three of us hope you will hold on to a phrase at-
tributed to the great Christian radical Jacques Ellul: "Think
globally, act locally." But the reverse is true as well. You have to
learn to "act globally and think locally." This means allowing
global circumstances to motivate your local actions, and the
relational fidelity you learn at the local level to motivate your
global actions. It is this prayerful practice of both movements
that holds so much unexplored possibility.

You simply cannot go around claiming faith in the beauty of

God's vision of shalom and forget about the quality of your rooted and linked relationships. If you lean into the famous charge of Abraham Kuyper that "there is not a square inch in the whole domain of our human existence over which Christ . . . does not cry, Mine!" then you must begin living generously and faithfully as if this were true.

Suppose that the three of us had the willing ear of the White House, or even the United Nations. Uh . . . unlikely. We know. But if we were asked for a prescription for global change, would our message be any different to them? Bearing context in mind, not really. Once you believe that change happens by learning how to be faithfully present to each other, then you need a place where you can practice trusting God to make it real at an *everyday* level.

Does this mean that you shouldn't be concerned about the specific reforms needed in, say, education or generating civil discourse in politics or a marketplace that takes into consideration environmental justice and human rights? No! Of course you need to engage around the critical issues and industries to which you are called. But you don't want a bunch of people fighting for opposing agendas who have never learned to be faithful with their neighbors. And, of course, reforms aren't actually reforms unless they enable real people to live more faithfully together with one another and with the created world. We need a platform where it all belongs and it's all connected relationally.

Niche issues and awareness campaigns are important, but surely these mobilizations for change will not be sustained if all that holds them together are short bursts of attention. As mentioned before, what's so desperately needed today in both the church and the broader public square is a new imagination for connecting the particular to the universal, the local to the global.

An individualistic and consumerist society will always be pushing the "issue of the month" into the spotlight. The task is to find a way forward that acknowledges the specific insight of particular issues while at the same time creating space to see the whole. You gotta roll up your sleeves and do your part in the core work of identifying, connecting and encouraging long-term faith communities within the parish and networking these communities together.

Unfortunately, a false dichotomy exists when it comes to networks and movements that truly embrace either the local or the global. So many of the local movements, like eating-local initiatives, small business alliances and robust neighborhood councils, can be suspicious of anything that's not explicitly local. In an increasingly networked globe this is an unwise posture. In fact, more often than not, it actually hurts the vision of remaining a stable presence of local responsibility.

Sometimes the best catalyst for local responsibility is actually taking pilgrimages to other local places. Learning from other places, other systems and other complexities not only broadens your understanding of the world, it gives you greater insight into your own place.

Now, the reverse is certainly true for global organizations and "grand movements." While global interconnectivity is a powerful way to learn about new ideas and cultures, there are key insights that only come from relationships at the local level. It might not be as explicit, but the local "small stuff" is often overlooked, and can be seen as insignificant. When your mindset is oriented around scaling exponential growth, local communities are treated more like an outpost for a global brand than as an intricate part of the whole. As a result, indigenous, incarnational and truly relational ways of working together are viewed as too slow and cumbersome.

Indeed, when the global is set up to be over and against the local it's often a sign of a "power over" attitude. Of course, the same goes for the other direction. Putting the local over and against the global is also a sign of misguided thinking. Both the localist and the globalist can institute techniques of avoidance as they seek to defend their side. The obvious solution is, of course, to find as many ways as possible to develop deep reciprocity between the local and the global.

THE AGE TO COME

It's impossible to imagine what the church will look and feel like in the next ten years, much less in the next fifty. But an educated guess would propose these localizing and globalizing movements will continue to grow. While volumes could be written on these converging forces, we feel confident God is at work in a new way. The opportunity to be the church in our day, with all of the various challenges and possibilities in a radically changing world is breathtaking. From neighborhood to neighborhood and city to city we truly believe the Spirit is up to something profound. Our great hope is to be a small part of it. We think that it's your hope as well.

If you're reading this you've stuck with us to the end of the book. My, how we'd love to hear what is stirring within you! The overwhelming response we've received from people in our own parishes, from our parish tours and from our teaching on the new parish has been a profound sense that the Spirit is on the move. But how people feel after seeing and hearing these changes can vary quite a bit:

- We hear from some that Christianity is shifting from ideas and beliefs to a new way of living life.

- Some people now realize they had subtly bought into the lie that their Christian community was somehow in competition with other churches in their place.

- Others discovered they had inadvertently reduced following Jesus to certain spiritual disciplines that are too distant from the real physical world.

- We have also heard from those who feel overwhelmed or who feel that the shift is too radical.

- One of the most difficult situations we hear about is the feeling that one's current pattern of life is so fragmented that they can scarcely imagine how to begin.

- A few even feel that what we're advocating is threatening to their understanding and practice of church.

While these concerns feel very real, and we seek to honor these feelings, we want to encourage you to discern a practice or two as a means of "trying it on." Whether you are thrilled or terrified by what you've read, it is our hope that you and a few others will spur each other on to experiment in your neighborhood. It is in practicing your faith that the impossible begins to open up. It is in developing small, doable rhythms and rituals that reconnect your faith to everyday life and that open doors in ways you might never have expected.

Christine and Tom Sine, founders of Mustard Seed Associates, have been pioneering mentors to the three of us. For decades they have led the way, helping people risk living into a vibrant faith. In the final chapter of one of Christine's many wonderful writings she offers these words, "I believe God has placed within all of us 'impossible dreams' that we are called to bring into reality on earth—dreams that will bring glimpses of God's shalom world into people's lives."[1] But these dreams are not things we wring out of the world through superhuman efforts to add-on, or force upon our already busy lives. As Christine and Tom often remind us, these dreams are gifts we receive through entering into God's "shalom rhythms." These are patterns of prayer, rest, celebration, play, and yes, work—but work that is within the bounds of both our human limitations and responsibilities.

And you are not alone. As you take brave steps of faith, we want to leave you with a benediction from Jesus, who is the very center of our hope. It's a simple reminder and a profound dare: "Peace be with you! As the Father has sent me, I am sending you" (John 20:21).

Jesus spoke these words to his followers in the days between his resurrection and ascension. You've likely heard these words many times in your life. They are powerful words. Words challenging our modes of ministry and visions of success. If you're like us, there are moments when you wish that Jesus had sent us differently than the Father sent him. After all, the Father sent Jesus embodied in humble obscurity, with real limitations based on his family, culture and occupied state. Jesus was sent as a person with certain responsibilities that were his to own.

Jesus was sent to be faithfully present. And it cost him his life; which is to say he found his life in giving it up. There might be times when you wish Jesus had said, "Success be with you. While the Father sent me to be faithfully present, I am sending you to fix the world." But that's not who God is. This kind of renewal works from the inside out. And this includes places as much as persons. So please, as a parting blessing, don't forget what Jesus promised you. It's a promise he makes to each and every one of us: "I'll be with you as you do this, day after day after day, right up to the end of the age" (Matthew 28:20 *The Message*).

NEW PARISH PRAYER

Alpha and Omega, Beginning and End,

Even as we come to the end of this book may you begin reshaping our imagination for the neighborhood you have called us to. May we integrate mission, community and discipleship into a life that holistically worships you. Help us to follow Jesus into our neighborhood, together, and for your glory.

Amen.

Gratitudes

Gratitude unlocks the fullness of life.
It turns what we have into enough, and more.
It turns denial into acceptance, chaos to order, confusion to clarity.
It can turn a meal into a feast, a house into a home,
a stranger into a friend.

Melody Beattie

The essence of all beautiful art, all great art, is gratitude.

Friedrich Nietzsche

We offer this book to you with hearts filled with gratitude. Many thanks to all of you for picking up this volume and offering your time and energy to engage it with fellow sojourners who long to join Christ in the place you are called.

We offer thanks . . .

For all those women and men who have come before us, who have lived lives of faithful presence within their time and place.

For local churches from every stream of Christian tradition who are living with, listening to and loving their neighbors as though they are encountering Christ.

For those leaders who choose to deepen roots in urban, suburban and rural places, staying even in the face of systemic economic injustice.

For the daring ones acting on the conviction that in the everyday stuff of life God provides what is needed for mission, community, formation as a life of worship.

We offer thanks . . .

For the parish leaders, partners and friends who both encourage us and remind us of the beauty of lives well lived in place—for Alexia Salvatierra, Brenda Salter McNeil, Christina Cleveland, Carolyn Christmas, Noel Castellanos, Shane Claiborne, Adam McLane, Becky Tucker, Brian Boitmann, Chris Smith, Christy Tennant Krispin, Karen Wilk, John Pattison, Cameron Roxburgh, Tim Dickau, Michelle Hildebrand, Martin Robinson, Wendy McCaig, Sherry and Geoff Maddock, Kevin Rains, Rosa Lee Harden, Steve Knight, Lisa Sharon Harper, Pamela Wilhelms, Scott Cripps, Jeff and Kristy Dyer, Rob Yackley, Kirk Lauckner, Christiana Chase Rice, Craig Goodwin, Darin Petersen, David Leong, Holly Knoll, Jamie Taylor, Josh Harper, Jim Padilla Deborst, Jimmy Spencer Jr., John Pattison, Jon Huckins, JR Woodward, Karlene Clark, Kristy Dyer, Leroy Barber, Lisa Etter Carlson, Lon Wong, Mark Votava, Rebecca Lujan Loveless, Holly Knoll, Rosa Lee Harden, Ruth Padilla Deborst, Ryan Marsh, Sean Gladding, Steve Knight, Tony Kriz, Andy Wade, Micah Bournes, Scott and Jolynn Davison, and the late Richard Twiss.

For the Inhabit Conference dreamers Cathy Loerzel, Jeanette White, Trishelle Edwards, Josue Blanco, Brian Schroeder, Daniel Tidwell, Jason Best, Morgan Schmidt, Natasha Hicks, Jessica Ketola, Ron Ruthruff, Eileen Suico, Martin Robinson, and the dozens volunteers and sponsors, and hundreds of co-conspirators who breathe life into this gathering.

We offer thanks . . .

For the women and men who so graciously sharpened our articulation of the themes of this book through the Leadership in the New Parish Certificate—for Kirk Lauckner, Kate Willette, Jordan Serracino, Justin Gresham, Cary Umhau, Dan Oberg, Bruce Hanson, Sean Hall, Ed Jager, Ron Vanden Brink, Daniel McCarthy, Mark Votava, Al Doyle, Graham McMahon, Jessica Ketola, Glen Soderholm, Elizabeth Sparks, Todd Rubie, Brian Bajari, Charis Weathers, Jodi Theut, Andrew Tarrant, Amy Lauckner, John Pattison, Marc Powell, Jorge Tovar, Tasha Hicks, Eileen Suico, Rich Sclafani, Greg Diloreto.

For those who believed and invested in this practitioners' think-tank—for the Murdock Foundation, Keith Anderson, Derek McNeil, The Seattle School board of directors, Cathy Loerzel, Trishelle Edwards, Nicole Greenwald, Rachael Clinton.

We offer thanks . . .

For the team at InterVarsity Press who believed in this project even before a word was on the page—especially for Dave Zimmerman, Andrew Bronson, Adrianna Wright and Nathan Baker-Lutz—and for all the innovation and inspiration of leaders who have collaborated with us through the Parish Collective and The Seattle School.

GRATITUDE FROM PAUL

To the guides who have given me courage and inspiration, special thanks to Michael Frost, Majora Carter, Jim Diers, Milenko Matanovic, Al Roxburgh, Esther Meek, Karen Ward, The Sines, Mark Scandrette, Ruth Padilla Deborst, Candy Chang, Patricia Talton, Dave Hillis, Dr. Perkins, Travis Reed and Jonathan Wilson-Hartgrove.

To my fellow sojourners who have borne the weight of my

explorations over the years with genuine friendship and courage, special thanks to Mike and Molly Ott, Mark Votava, Nichole and Danny Connelly, Holly Knoll, Justin Mayfield, Josh and Melina Ott, Nick & Nora Leider, Melody & Ben Smith, Jason and Anna Ott, Ian McMurren, Justin Crockett, Gary Waldron, Jennifer Suggs, Daniel Blue, Christy Stolz, Gary and Denise Hansen, and Eunice Galvez.

To my dear mother and family, and, finally, to my wife Elizabeth Sparks, the love and inspiration of my life.

GRATITUDE FROM TIM

For Dr. Randy Rowland of the Christian Reformed Church for nurturing these ideas at the seedling stage, and the courageous crew who joined the team with hopes of bringing heaven to earth in South Lake Union.

For Ben and Cherie Katt, and Lisa and Andy Carlson, thank you for your friendship, your encouragement and your embodiment of this book.

For my friends eating soup and caring for kids together in Wallingford, and the delightful welcome of Elim Baptist Church, especially pastor Mick Berberian for over thirty years of faithful presence.

For my parents, Dave and Jane Soerens, not only their constant support, but for allowing the space to live my questions.

Finally, for my son Lukas who fills my life with light, and especially for my wife Maria Jose, thank you for your courage, your brilliance and your abiding love. My heart is filled with gratitude.

GRATITUDE FROM DWIGHT

For my friends in Lake Hills who are transforming a Seattle suburb into a place of shared life we can all call home . . .

For my colleagues at The Seattle School of Theology & Psychology who faithfully invite my presence . . .

For the women and men I get to study with day in and day out, especially the students in that first class on the new parish: Jonathan Adams, Dan Brown, Knox Burnett, Morgan Schmidt, Bitta Fynskov Clark, Eric Nicolaysen, David Von Stroh and Johnny Wakefield . . .

For my family: Dad and Mom Friesen, Michelle and Ken, Dallas and Leanne, Dad and Mom Klassen, Bevan and Carolyn, and the great cloud of witnesses that are my uncles, aunts, cousins, nephews and nieces . . .

Lastly, for Lynette and Pascal, who invite me into wonder, shepherd me into the real and woo me to love . . . My heart is filled with gratitude.

GRATITUDE FOR FRIENDSHIP

For each other: the three of us have been living, playing, collaborating, writing, arguing, teaching, grieving, visiting neighborhoods, encouraging and loving one another for a while now. Our hearts are filled with gratitude.

Thanks again for picking up *The New Parish*; we'd love to from you and learn about your parish. Come visit us at www .newparish.org.

NEW PARISH PRAYER

Creator God,

Thank you for the gift of life. Grant us eyes to see the people, places, and gifts with which you fill our lives moment by moment, such that we become people of deep gratitude.

Amen.

Recommended Resources

CHAPTER 1: DISLOCATED

Gorringe, Timothy J. *A Theology of the Built Environment: Justice, Empowerment, Redemption*. Cambridge, UK: Cambridge University Press, 2002.

McKnight, John, and Peter Block. *The Abundant Community: Awakening the Power of Families and Neighborhoods*. San Francisco: Barrett-Koehler Publishers, 2010.

Roxburgh, Alan J. *Missional: Joining God in the Neighborhood*. Grand Rapids: Baker Books, 2011.

CHAPTER 2: MISPLACED

Brueggemann, Walter. *Journey to the Common Good*. Louisville, KY: Westminster John Knox, 2010.

Hunter, James Davison. *To Change the World: The Irony, Tragedy, and Possibility of Christianity in the Late Modern World*. New York: Oxford University Press, 2010.

Spretnak, Charlene. *The Resurgence of the Real: Body, Nature, and Place in a Hypermodern World*. New York: Routledge, 1999.

CHAPTER 3: FAITHFUL PRESENCE

Bartholomew, Craig G. *Where Mortals Dwell: A Christian View of Place for Today*. Grand Rapids: Baker Academic, 2011.

Dickau, Tim. *Plunging into the Kingdom Way: Practicing the Shared Strokes of Community, Hospitality, Justice, and Confession*. Eugene, OR: Cascade Books, 2011.

Jacobsen, Eric O. *Sidewalks in the Kingdom: New Urbanism and the Christian Faith*. Grand Rapids: Brazos Press, 2003.

Stark, Rodney. *Cities of God: The Real Story of How Christianity Became an Urban Movement and Conquered Rome*. New York: HarperOne, 2007.

Stegemann, Ekkehard, and Wolfgang Stegemann. *The Jesus Movement: A Social History of Its First Century*. Minneapolis: Fortress Press, 1999.

CHAPTER 4: ECCLESIAL CENTER

Block, Peter. *Community: The Structure of Belonging*. San Francisco: Barrett-Koehler, 2008.

Bosch, David J. *Transforming Mission: Paradigm Shifts in Theology of Mission*. Maryknoll, NY: Orbis Books, 1991.

Bouma-Prediger, Steven, and Brian J. Walsh. *Beyond Homelessness: Christian Faith in a Culture of Displacement*. Grand Rapids: Eerdmans, 2008.

Labberton, Mark. *The Dangerous Act of Loving Your Neighbor: Seeing Others Through the Eyes of Jesus*. Downers Grove, IL: InterVarsity Press, 2010.

Scandrette, Mark. *Practicing the Way of Jesus: Life Together in the Kingdom of Love*. Downers Grove, IL: InterVarsity Press, 2011.

Smith, James K. A. *Desiring the Kingdom: Worship Worldview, and Cultural Formation*. Grand Rapids: Baker Academic, 2009.

CHAPTER 5: NEW COMMONS

Cortese, Amy. *Locavesting: The Revolution in Local Investing and How to Profit from It*. Hoboken, NJ: John Wiley, 2011.

Jacobsen, Eric O. *The Space Between: A Christian Engagement with the Built Environment*. Grand Rapids: Baker Academic, 2012.

Reid, Herbert, and Betsy Taylor. *Recovering the Commons: Democracy, Place, and Global Justice*. Urbana: University of Illinois Press, 2010.

Salvatierra, Alexia, and Peter Heltzel. *Faith-Rooted Organizing: Mobi-*

lizing the Church in Service to the World. Downers Grove, IL: Inter-
Varsity Press, 2013.

Walljasper, Jay. All That We Share: How to Save the Economy, the Environment, the Internet, Democracy, Our Communities and Everything
Else That Belongs to All of Us. New York: New Press, 2010.

CHAPTER 6: PRESENCING

Heifetz, Ronald, Alexander Grashow and Marty Linsky. The Practice of
Adaptive Leadership. Cambridge, MA: Harvard Business Press, 2009.

Meek, Esther Lightcap. Loving to Know: Covenant Epistemology. Eugene,
OR: Cascade Books, 2011.

Sine, Christine, and Tom Sine. Living on Purpose: Finding God's Best for
Your Life. Grand Rapids: Baker Books, 2002.

Smith, James K. A. Imagining the Kingdom: How Worship Works. Grand
Rapids: Baker Academic, 2013.

CHAPTER 7: ROOTING

Brueggemann, Walter. The Land: Place as Gift, Promise, and Challenge
in Biblical Faith. Minneapolis: Fortress, 1997.

Frost, Michael, and Alan Hirsch. The Shaping of Things to Come: Innovation and Mission for the 21st-Century Church. Peabody, MA: Hendrickson, 2003.

Gordon, Wayne, and John Perkins. Making Neighborhoods Whole: A
Handbook for Christian Community Development. Downers Grove,
IL: InterVarsity Press, 2013.

Walljasper, Jay. The Great Neighborhood Book: A Do-It-Yourself Guide to
Placemaking. Gabriola, BC: New Society Publishers, 2007.

Wilson-Hartgrove, Jonathan. The Wisdom of Stability: Rooting Faith in
a Mobile Culture. Brewster, MA: Paraclete Press, 2010.

CHAPTER 8: LINKING

Cleveland, Christena. Disunity in Christ: Uncovering the Hidden Forces
That Keep Us Apart. Downers Grove, IL: InterVarsity Press, 2013.

Friesen, Dwight J. *Thy Kingdom Connected.* Grand Rapids: Baker Books, 2009.

Pohl, Christine D. *Living into Community: Cultivating Practices That Sustain Us.* Grand Rapids: Eerdmans, 2012.

Sine, Tom. *The New Conspirators: Creating the Future One Mustard Seed at a Time.* Downers Grove, IL: InterVarsity Press, 2008.

Tharp, Twyla, and Jesse Kornbluth. *The Collaborative Habit: Life Lessons for Working Together.* New York: Simon & Schuster, 2009.

Twiss, Richard. *One Church, Many Tribes: Following Jesus the Way God Made You.* Ventura, CA: Regal Books, 2000.

CHAPTER 9: LEADING

Griffin, Douglas. *The Emergence of Leadership: Linking Self-Organization and Ethics.* New York: Routledge, 2002.

Newbigin, Lesslie. *The Gospel in a Pluralist Society.* Grand Rapids: Eerdmans, 1989.

Parks, Sharon Daloz. *Leadership Can Be Taught: A Bold Approach for a Complex World.* Boston: Harvard Business School Press, 2005.

Glossary of Terms

New Parish Language House

adaptive presencing. To face complex situations for which there is no technical fix while attuned to the Spirit's guidance through the ongoing cycle of listening, discerning and acting together.

ecclesial center. Becoming the church in the parish together by integrating formation, community and mission as your common life of worship (faithful presence).

faithful presence. Entering into your present circumstance responsive to both your limitations and responsibilities for relating to God, to others and to the created world.

leadership. The capacity to mobilize a group's desire for reconciliation and renewal through collective action, while paying ongoing attention to God's story, to the fidelity of the group within its place and to the leader's own transformation.

linking. The practice of developing meaningful connections with people and places outside of your own parish.

narrative braid. The intertwining of the gospel story, your personal narrative and the story of the place you inhabit to form a rubric for discerning your active engagement in the parish.

neighborhood. *See* parish.

new commons. The dimensions of life for which everyone in your neighborhood shares a common concern (categories include economy, environment, education and civic).

new parish. A parish where there are diverse church expressions living out their faith together as one local body that is linked across parishes, growing the unity of one church.

new parish church. All the people within a parish who practice following Jesus together.

parish. All the relationships in the place where the local church lives out its faith together (God, others, geography, etc.).

rooting. The practice of becoming a familiar character within the ongoing story of your parish.

spatial blindness. The condition of being unable to see or interpret reality because of a lack of either rooted relations or linking connections.

Notes

INTRODUCTION

[1]Michael Frost and Alan Hirsch, *The Shaping of Things to Come: Innovation and Mission for the 21st-Century Church* (Peabody, MA: Hendrickson, 2003).

CHAPTER 1: DISLOCATED

[1]See Ferris Jabr, "How Brainless Slime Molds Redefine Intelligence," *Scientific American,* November 7, 2012, accessed December 17, 2013, at www.scientificamerican.com/article.cfm?id=brainless-slime-molds.

[2]Eva Feder Kittay, *The Subject of Care: Feminist Perspective on Dependency* (New York: Rowman & Littlefield, 2002), p. 354.

[3]Parker Palmer, *The Courage to Teach: Exploring the Inner Landscape of a Teacher's Life* (San Francisco: Jossey-Bass, 2007), p. 100.

[4]Christena Cleveland, *Disunity in Christ: Uncovering the Hidden Forces That Keep Us Apart* (Downers Grove, IL: InterVarsity Press, 2013), p. 26.

[5]Shane Claiborne, *The Irresistible Revolution: Living as an Ordinary Radical* (Grand Rapids: Zondervan, 2006).

[6]"Small Seeds, Real Places, and the Gospel: A Conversation with Shane Claiborne," Parish Collective, August 18, 2011, http://vimeo.com/27850420.

CHAPTER 2: MISPLACED

[1]Kanye West and Jay Z, www.youtube.com/watch?v=FJt7gNi3Nr4, accessed November 21, 2013.

[2]We are indebted to Leroy Barber for the new parish connection to this Kanye West and Jay Z song. At the 2013 Inhabit Conference in Seattle, Leroy a delivered a powerful keynote address titled "Church in the Wild."

[3]For a helpful exploration of "faithful presence" see James Davison Huntor, *To Change the World: The Irony, Tragedy, and Possibility of Christianity in the Late Modern World* (New York: Oxford University Press, 2010), p. 95.

[4]Rodney Stark, *Cities of God: The Real Story of How Christianity Became an*

Urban Movement and Conquered Rome (New York: HarperCollins, 2009), p. 26.

[5]Ibid., p. 13.

[6]"Dr. John Perkins on the Gospel, community and the neighborhood," Parish Collective, November 23, 2010, https://vimeo.com/17108561.

[7]Thomas Long, *Accompany Them with Singing: The Christian Funeral* (Louisville, KY: Westminster John Knox, 2009).

[8]Latin for "and [from] the Son," this phrase is found in the form of the Nicene Creed used in most Western churches. It is not present in the Greek text of the Nicene Creed as originally formulated at the First Council of Constantinople, which says only that the Holy Spirit proceeds "from the Father."

[9]Donald A. McGavran, *Understanding Church Growth* (Grand Rapids: Eerdmans, 1990).

[10]Lesslie Newbigin, *The Gospel in a Pluralist Society* (Grand Rapids: Eerdmans, 1989), p. 119.

CHAPTER 3: FAITHFUL PRESENCE

[1]Elizabeth Newman, *Untamed Hospitality* (Grand Rapids: Brazos Press, 2007), p. 97.

[2]Richard Cavel, *McLuhan in Space: A Cultural Geography* (Toronto: University of Toronto Press, 2003), p. 96.

[3]Bob Dylan, "Gotta Serve Somebody," *Slow Train Coming* (1979).

[4]Eric Jacobsen, *The Space Between: A Christian Engagement with the Built Environment* (Grand Rapids: Baker Academic, 2012), p. 83.

[5]Jacques Ellul, *The Technological Society* (New York: Alfred A. Knopf, 1964), p. 11.

[6]James C. Scott, *Seeing Like a State* (New Haven, CT: Yale University Press, 1998), p. 13.

[7]Jean-Paul Sartre, *Saint Genet: Actor and Martyr* (Minneapolis: University of Minnesota Press, 2012), p. 213.

[8]Mark Van Steenwyk, *The Unkingdom of God: Embracing the Subversive Power of Repentance* (Downers Grove, IL: InterVarsity Press, 2013), p. 45.

[9]Dietrich Bonhoeffer, *Life Together* (New York: HarperOne, 1978), p. 17.

[10]Mark Scandrette, *Practicing the Way of Jesus* (Downers Grove, IL: InterVarsity Press, 2011), p. 18.

CHAPTER 4: ECCLESIAL CENTER

[1]Alan Roxburgh, *Missional: Joining God in the Neighborhood* (Grand Rapids: Baker Books, 2011), p. 65.

[2]Michael Warren, *At This Time, in This Place: The Spirit Embodied in the Local Assembly* (Philadelphia: Trinity Press International, 1999), p. 17.

[3]See Tony Kriz, "Do Small: A Short Feature on a Parish Orientation," http://tonykriz.com/?p=407, accessed November 13, 2013.

[4]Dietrich Bonhoeffer, *Life Together* (New York: Harper & Row, 1954), pp. 27-28.

[5]James K. A. Smith, *Desiring the Kingdom: Worship, Worldview, and Cultural Formation* (Grand Rapids: Baker Academic, 2009), p. 37.

CHAPTER 5: NEW COMMONS

[1]Dietrich Bonhoeffer, "The church is the church only when it exists for others," *Letters and Papers from Prison* (New York: Touchstone, 1997).

[2]Jay Walljasper, *All That We Share: How to Save the Economy, the Environment, the Internet, Democracy, Our Communities and Everything Else That Belongs to All of Us* (New York: New Press, 2010).

[3]Pamela Wilhelms, conversation with the authors, April 24-25, 2013.

[4]John McKnight and Peter Block, *The Abundant Community* (San Francisco: Berrett-Koehler, 2010), p. 1.

[5]Alvin Troffler and Heidi Toffler, *Revolutionary Wealth: How It Will Be Created and How It Will Change Our Lives* (New York: Doubleday, 2006), p. 155.

[6] "About Us," Business Alliance for Local Living Economies, http://bealocalist.org/bailes-guiding-vision, accessed November 14, 2013.

[7]Walter Brueggemann, *The Land: Place as Gift, Promise, and Challenge in Biblical Faith* (Minneapolis: Augsburg Fortress, 2002), p. 3.

[8]Howard A. Snyder with Joel Scandrett, *Salvation Means Creation Healed: The Ecology of Sin and Grace: Overcoming the Divorce Between Earth and Heaven* (Eugene, OR: Wipf and Stock, 2011).

[9]Bill McKibben, *Oil and Honey: The Education of an Unlikely Activist* (New York: Times Books, 2013).

[10]Norman Wirzba, ed. *The Art of the Commonplace: The Agrarian Essays of Wendell Berry* (Berkeley, CA: Counterpoint, 2002).

[11]Ivan Illich, *Tools for Conviviality* (London: Marion Boyars, 1973), p. 50.

[12]Chris Smith and John Pattison, *Slow Church: Cultivating Community in the*

Patient Way of Jesus (Downers Grove, IL: InterVarsity Press, 2014), pp. 14-15.

[13]Brueggemann, *The Land*, p. 4.

[14]Harlem Children's Zone, "About Geoffrey Canada," http://hcz.org/index.php/about-us/about-geoffrey-canada, accessed November 14, 2013.

[15]Daniel Kemmis, *Community and the Politics of Place* (Norman: University of Oklahoma Press, 1990), pp. 79-80.

CHAPTER 6: PRESENCING

[1]Ann Morisy, *Bothered and Bewildered: Enacting Hope in Troubled Times* (New York: Bloomsbury Academic, 2008).

[2]Ursula Franklin, *The Ursula Franklin Reader* (Toronto: Between the Lines, 2006), p. 214.

[3]Marva Dawn, *Unfettered Hope: A Call to Faithful Living in an Affluent Society* (Louisville, KY: Westminster John Knox, 2003), p. 4.

[4]Craig G. Bartholomew and Michael W. Goheen, *The Drama of Scripture: Finding Our Place in the Biblical Story* (Grand Rapids: Baker Academic, 2004), p. 208.

[5]Daniel Taylor, *Tell Me a Story: The Life-Shaping Power of Our Stories* (St. Paul, MN: Bog Walk Press, 2001), p. 1.

[6]Dan B. Allender, *To Be Told: Know Your Story, Shape Your Future* (Colorado Springs: Waterbrook, 2005), p. 1.

[7]Wendell Berry, "Wendell Berry on His Hopes for Humanity," interview with Bill Moyers, October 4, 2013, http://billmoyers.com/segment/wendell-berry-on-his-hopes-for-humanity/.

[8]Jamie Arpin-Ricci, *The Cost of Community: Jesus, St. Francis and Life in the Kingdom* (Downers Grove, IL: InterVarsity Press, 2011), p. 46.

[9]Inspired by the most recent work of John McKnight and Peter Block in their excellent book, *The Abundant Community: Awakening the Power of Families and Neighborhoods* (San Francisco: Berrett-Koehler, 2012).

[10]Trevor Robb, "Highlands to Spearhead Abundant Communities Initiative Pilot," February 11, 2013, *Edmonton Examiner*, www.edmontonexaminer.com/2013/02/06/highlands-to-spearhead-abundant-communities-initiative-pilot.

CHAPTER 7: ROOTING

[1]Jonathan Wilson-Hartgrove, *The Wisdom of Stability: Rooting Faith in a Mobile Culture* (Brewster, MA: Paraclete Press, 2010), p. 1.

[2]Wendell Berry, quoting E. M. Forster, "It All Turns on Affection," 2012 Jefferson lecture, National Endowment for the Humanities, www.neh.gov/about/awards/jefferson-lecture/wendell-e-berry-lecture, accessed November 12, 2013.

[3]Jon Tyson, *Sacred Roots: Why Church Still Matters in a Post-Religious Era* (Grand Rapids: Zondervan, 2014).

[4]Tony Kriz, *Neighbors and Wisemen* (Nashville: Thomas Nelson, 2011), p. 225.

[5]David Abram, *The Spell of the Sensuous* (New York: Pantheon, 1996), p. 181.

[6]Charlene Spretnak, *The Resurgence of the Real: Body, Nature and Place in a Hypermodern World* (New York: Routledge, 1999), pp. 2, 4.

[7]Personal conversation with the authors and Brandon Rhodes, April 14, 2013.

CHAPTER 8: LINKING

[1]Marva Dawn, *Unfettered Hope: A Call to Faithful Living in an Affluent Society* (Louisville, KY: Westminster John Knox, 2003), p. 8.

[2]Paul Virilio, *The Information Bomb* (New York: Verso, 2005), pp. 15, 21.

[3]C. S. Lewis, *God in the Dock: Essays on Theology and Ethics* (Grand Rapids: Eerdmans, 1970), pp. 201-2.

CHAPTER 9: LEADING

[1]Dan White Jr., quoted from twitter.com, @danwhitejr.

[2]Ronald A. Heifetz, *Leadership Without Easy Answers* (Cambridge, MA: Harvard University Press, 1994), pp. 13-14.

[3]Patricia Talton, *Wisdom as a Means to Transformation*, www.youtube.com/watch?v=QnfN0nC-AqI, accessed November 13, 2013.

[4]Sharon Daloz Parks, "Preskill and Brookfield's Nine Learning Tasks of Leadership," North Seattle Community College, Fall 2009.

[5]Michael Frost, *Incarnate: The Body of Christ in an Age of Disengagement* (Downers Grove, IL: InterVarsity Press, 2014), p. 155.

CONCLUSION

[1]Christine Sine, *Sacred Rhythms: Finding a Peaceful Pace in a Hectic World* (Grand Rapids: Baker Books, 2003), p. 226.

PARISH COLLECTIVE
ROOTED AND LINKED

Parish Collective connects and resources people of faith in particular neighborhoods to be the church together in the place they live. When we share our stories, connections and resources in and across parishes, it helps weave together neighborhood churches, missional communities and any group of Christ-followers that desires renewal in their neighborhood.

Go to **parishcollective.org** to

- find hundreds of neighborhood renewal stories
- collaborate with others in your area through our online map
- discover support for growing parish expressions in the place you live

---

IVP PRAXIS
EQUIPPING LEADERS FOR MINISTRY

If you are called to ministry, you know you can't do it on your own. Let Praxis provide the companions you need to equip God's people for life in the kingdom.

www.ivpress.com/praxis

The Seattle School
OF THEOLOGY & PSYCHOLOGY

The formation of The Seattle School of Theology & Psychology began around a kitchen table, where a gathering of a few passionate dreamers dared to imagine a new kind of theological, psychological and cultural training. As we have listened to and joined God's movement in the kingdom and in our own local context, we have come to claim the new parish model as the hope for the future of the church.

The Seattle School is becoming a hub for new parish thought leadership. We are cultivating contexts for gathering that inspire, support and equip parish leaders through our Inhabit Conference and new parish gatherings and workshops. Through the leadership of Paul Sparks, Tim Soerens and Dwight J. Friesen, we are equipping parish practitioners through our **Leadership in the New Parish Certificate**. We are also cultivating and training a new generation of leaders through parish-oriented pathways within our **Master of Arts in Theology & Culture** and **Master of Divinity** programs.

Join us and learn more at **theseattleschool.edu**.